Playing and Becoming in Psychoanalysis

Building on Winnicott's theory of play, this book defines the concept of play from the perspective of clinical practice, elaborating on its application to clinical problems.

Although Winnicott's theory of play constitutes a radical understanding of the intersubjectivity of therapy, Cooper contends, there remains a need to explore the significance of play to the enactment of transference-countertransference. Among several ideas, this book considers how to help patients as they navigate debilitating internal object relations, supporting them to engage with "bad objects" in alternatively playful ways. In addition, throughout the book, Cooper develops an ethic of play that can support the analyst to find "ventilated spaces" of their own, whereby they can reflect on transference-countertransference. Rather than being hindered by the limits of the therapeutic setting, this book explores how possibilities for play can develop out of these very constraints, ultimately providing a fulsome exploration of the concept without eviscerating its magic.

With a broad theoretical base, and a wide definition of play, this book will appeal to psychoanalysts and psychoanalytic psychotherapists wanting to understand how play functions within and can transform their clinical practice.

Steven H. Cooper is a training and supervising analyst at the Boston Psychoanalytic Society and Institute. He is on the faculty at the New York University Postdoctoral Program in Psychoanalysis and Psychotherapy and the Austen Riggs Center. He is in private practice in New York.

Psychoanalysis in a New Key Book Series

Series Editor: Donnel Stern

When music is played in a new key, the melody does not change, but the notes that make up the composition do: change in the context of continuity, continuity that perseveres through change. Psychoanalysis in a New Key publishes books that share the aims psychoanalysts have always had, but that approach them differently. The books in the series are not expected to advance any particular theoretical agenda, although to this date most have been written by analysts from the Interpersonal and Relational orientations.

The most important contribution of a psychoanalytic book is the communication of something that nudges the reader's grasp of clinical theory and practice in an unexpected direction. Psychoanalysis in a New Key creates a deliberate focus on innovative and unsettling clinical thinking. Because that kind of thinking is encouraged by exploration of the sometimes surprising contributions to psychoanalysis of ideas and findings from other fields, Psychoanalysis in a New Key particularly encourages interdisciplinary studies. Books in the series have married psychoanalysis with dissociation, trauma theory, sociology, and criminology. The series is open to the consideration of studies examining the relationship between psychoanalysis and any other field—for instance, biology, literary and art criticism, philosophy, systems theory, anthropology, and political theory.

But innovation also takes place within the boundaries of psychoanalysis, and Psychoanalysis in a New Key therefore also presents work that reformulates thought and practice without leaving the precincts of the field. Books in the series focus, for example, on the significance of personal values in psychoanalytic practice, on the complex interrelationship between the analyst's clinical work and personal life, on the consequences for the clinical situation when patient and analyst are from different cultures, and on the need for psychoanalysts to accept the degree to which they knowingly satisfy their own wishes during treatment hours, often to the patient's detriment.

A full list of all titles in this series is available at: https://www.routledge.com/Psychoanalysis-in-a-New-Key-Book-Series/book-series/LEAPNKBS

Playing and Becoming in Psychoanalysis

Steven Harlan Cooper

Routledge
Taylor & Francis Group

LONDON AND NEW YORK

Cover image: © Artwork by Jennifer Ellwood
(jenniferellwood.com)

First published 2023
by Routledge
4 Park Square, Milton Park, Abingdon, Oxon OX14 4RN

and by Routledge
605 Third Avenue, New York, NY 10158

Routledge is an imprint of the Taylor & Francis Group, an informa business

© 2023 Steven H. Cooper

British Library Cataloguing-in-Publication Data
A catalogue record for this book is available from the
British Library

Library of Congress Cataloging-in-Publication Data
Names: Cooper, Steven H., 1951- author.
Title: Playing and becoming in psychoanalysis / Steven Harlan Cooper.
Description: Abingdon, Oxon ; New York, NY : Routledge, 2022. |
Includes bibliographical references and index.
Identifiers: LCCN 2022003153 (print) | LCCN 2022003154
(ebook) | ISBN 9781032207544 (hardback) | ISBN
9781032207551 (paperback) | ISBN 9781003265078 (ebook)
Subjects: LCSH: Play--Psychological aspects. | Object relations
(Psychoanalysis) | Psychoanalysis.
Classification: LCC BF717 .C665 2022 (print) | LCC BF717
(ebook) | DDC 155.4/18--dc23/eng/20220524
LC record available at https://lccn.loc.gov/2022003153
LC ebook record available at https://lccn.loc.gov/2022003154

ISBN: 978-1-032-20754-4 (hbk)
ISBN: 978-1-032-20755-1 (pbk)
ISBN: 978-1-003-26507-8 (ebk)

DOI: 10.4324/9781003265078

Typeset in Times New Roman
by MPS Limited, Dehradun

For Gwen

Contents

Acknowledgments

I am grateful to Kenneth Corbett, Jennifer Ellwood, James Frosch, Adrienne Harris, Anton Kris, Lucy Lafarge, Christopher Lovett, Mark O'Connell, and Richard Zimmer. These friends have read many parts of this volume and offered invaluable observations and critiques. Emma Sunog was a wondeful editor. I am also grateful to some journal reviewers of a few of the chapters in this volume who stimulated my thinking and whose names are unknown to me. Sometimes these reviewers offer writers invaluable insights and they do so without a direct opportunity for the writer to offer thanks. So, thank you to all I've mentioned and those whom I've alluded to who remain nameless.

Credits List

Steven H. Cooper (2022) The Limits of Intimacy and the Intimacy of Limits: Play and the Internal Object. *Journal of the American Psychoanalytic Association* 70(2), [xxx] © 2022 by American Psychoanalytic Association, Reprinted by Permission of SAGE Publications.

Introduction

Winnicott's introduction of play as the central element of therapeutic action in psychoanalysis marked a seismic shift in psychoanalytic theory and practice. Seventy years later, we are still mining the implications of his creative and enriching contribution to understanding psychoanalytic process.

I wrote this book because I wanted to explore a theory of play that evolved from my clinical work over the years. I also wanted to develop some of the embedded, revolutionary ideas in Winnicott's theory of play that had not been explicitly identified in relation to clinical work. As much as Winnicott's theory of play marked a radical understanding of the intersubjective component of therapeutic action, I felt that clinically we could elaborate more on the relationship of play to transference-countertransference engagement and enactment.

With the concept of play as central to therapeutic action, Winnicott was asserting that while the unconscious is always rooted in the symbolic, it is also rooted in relation to the other. Similar to Bion's notion that the mind can only exist in relation to a group, Winnicott's assertion that there is no such thing as an infant summarized that the subject is intrinsically trans-individual. Even prior to the developed concept of enactment, Winnicott intuited that play is intrinsically interactive and immersive.

I also realized that I had been struggling for a long time to understand the relationship between the refractoriness of internalized bad objects (Fairbairn, 1958; Rosenfeld, 1987) and play. In many ways I believe that Winnicott's theory of play was always occurring in relation to internalized painful experience and I wanted to further explore this

DOI: 10.4324/9781003265078-1

idea. The relationship of play to internal object as what I call "play partner" is an important part of what I will explore in this book.

For those of us who find that play is fundamental to psychoanalysis, there are challenges in delineating how it functions quite specifically in our work. Winnicott (1968a, b) referred repeatedly to the problem of how to define play and seemed to resist very specific definitions of the concept. In many ways, this book's errand is to describe and interrogate play, without eviscerating too much of its magic. Put another way, I aim to play with Winnicott's tantalizing ambiguity about what is inside and what is outside through clinical examples and discussion about analytic process.

At the broadest of levels, play is a way of thinking about the very logic that underlies, enlivens, and makes possible psychoanalysis. At this level, an element of play functions continuously to sustain and work with a paradoxical reality in which things are real and not real at the same time (e.g. Parsons, 1999). If play operates continuously and is not just an intermittent dimension of analysis, then how do we define it and get at the particular ways it manifests itself? In illustrating particular clinical moments of play, how do we differentiate these moments from the continuous operation of play? Even more important, how is play a crucial means of shifting processes in the therapeutic action of analytic work?

There is a pull to think about many of the components that make analysis work through a lens of play. For example, we could say that cultivating metaphoric capacities in the patient is one of the levels at which play occurs in psychoanalysis. Consider the following humorous remark by Ferenczi, one that highlights a kind of leap in the analyst's imagination during much of analytic work. Ferenczi (2013) stated that:

> The derisive remark was once made against psychoanalysis that according to this doctrine, the unconscious sees a penis in every convex object and a vagina or anus in every concave one. I find that this sentence well characterizes the facts.
>
> (p. 193)

This remark gets at one kind of play that patient and analyst engage in. Patient and analyst require metaphors in order to speak of the mind and often how the body is represented in the mind. By saying that this observation well characterizes the "facts," Ferenczi is reversing figure and ground by placing confidence in metaphor in order to speak of the mind. The metaphorical becomes the factual. Ferenczi's use of the term "factual" is a form of play within the metaphoric turn since he trusts this form of truth as much as some more direct observation of reality. He is changing rules about what is fact and what is speculative. His comment reflects play in that a deep level of trust is required. It could be said that in psychoanalysis, patient and analyst take a "leap" of faith regarding the metaphorical. Discovering the existence of the human mind, infantile sexuality, and the concept of transference all involved leaps of faith.

Since Plato (360 B.C.) first observed children and animals playing, the "leap" has been one of the most frequently used metaphors to describe play. The notion of leaping features a sense of freedom and exuberance. Leaping also emphasizes a kind of boundary crossing at the core of play. For in play, rules are always shifting or at least potentially shifting. We leap for joy to celebrate freedom from constraint. We leap for joy when we are in love or when we see someone whom we have missed. Leaps of imagination mark explosive creativity.

Erikson (1950) highlighted Plato's conjecture that the model of genuine playfulness is the need of all young children to leap. Erikson emphasized that the significance of the "leap" is in the need to "test the leeway, allowed by given limits; to outdo and yet not escape gravity" (p. 17). Erikson is referring to that quality of play which involves the maintenance of the "precarious" position between reality and fantasy.

While Plato wrote about the importance of play for the child, he seemed to have an ambivalent position regarding the role of play in adulthood (e.g. Armand D'Angour, 2013, p. 293). Plato was inclined to consider play an unworthy activity for adults. He did however suggest that intellectual play in some form, as demonstrated in the dialectical banter of Socrates, could provide a stimulus to understanding.

In 1932, the Dutch anthropologist, John Huizinga (1932) presented a radically new understanding of play as an activity that exists only for its own sake. This idea was developed more recently by a cultural anthropologist, Steven Johnson (2016). According to Huizinga, play absorbs us in a way that can remove or mitigate uncertainty. For

Huizinga, an activity is play if we are absorbed and taken over by it. Play can render complexity more manageable even when it may involve elements of illusion. I would add that in the clinical context, play can also succinctly interrogate illusion itself and turn reductionistic conclusions on their head.

In fact, much of play often pivots around a kind of interesting and creative concreteness. This concreteness reduces complexity as part of the play. We are in a sense momentarily relieved of the complexity. We push complexity to the background, knowing full well that reality rests at close distance from the pivot point of play. This is another way to describe the illusory elements of play. In professional wrestling, the term kayfabe refers to **the practice of maintaining the illusion that everything is real**—including the scripted personas, rivalries, and storylines. This often extends beyond the in-match performance to other contexts, such as backstage footage and interviews. In fact, in one sense, play can be seen as a distraction from something complex even though it generally illuminates complexity in its own creative way. We could even say that we are all playing on borrowed time, a way that play distracts us from the inevitability of death even as it helps us to integrate loss and death.

Huizinga emphasized in various ways how much play has to exist outside of ordinary life. It is not that ordinary life is denied, since when we play, we are always conscious of the fact that the play is not real. The consequences of play, generally speaking, will not affect our lives outside the play.

Huizinga defined play as an activity in which rules are always changing. Those who are involved in play hold on to the idea that the rules of the game exist in the play space but do not upend the rules in other spaces. One of the most radical contributions that Huizinga made to the understanding of play was his notion that play is intrinsically gratifying. In a fascinating recent book by Steven Johnson (2016) on play, he challenges the notion that necessity is the mother of invention. While there is no doubt that many inventions grew out of the engineer's need to develop war machinery, plumbing, and city design, there were many other inventions in the areas of garment design, landscape architecture, color preferences, and robotics that are not easily explained by the theory that play and inventiveness emerge exclusively from necessity.

Johnson argues that human beings have always had a kind of primary need for play. Cultural anthropologists have also long argued about the intrinsic versus evolutionary value of art since the beginning of mankind. It is easy to imagine that the earliest cave paintings brought pleasure but also served various functions that we can imagine but not know about with certainty.

In this book, my focus is on the importance of play to the psychoanalytic process. Winnicott (1968a, 1968b), Parsons (1999, 2006), and Roussillon (2011) among others have elaborated on how the play framework is operating at a foundational level all the time in psychoanalysis. Contemporary Bionians such as Civaterese (2008a) focusing on the dream framework and dreaming the patient have suggested that dreaming and playing have substantial overlap. There are also interpersonal theorists such as Stern (1990, 2015) who have lent highly useful constructs and frameworks for thinking about therapeutic process, such as courting surprise and relational freedom, that have some overlap with what I and others term play.

In this volume, I decided that I wanted to take a different approach to play, one that went beyond its valid function as the undergirding of analytic process. I wanted to define play in relation to intersubjective engagement in specific clinical contexts, such as the role of play for patients who struggle with parental absence. I had learned that play sometimes emerges with patients who have resistance to mourning disappointing relations with others. I was also interested in the ethical foundation of play in the analytic situation. Yet, given the ways that play is foundational to the psychoanalytic process, I sought to define playing in psychoanalysis in ways that do not collapse its deep and irreducible role as the undergirding of analytic process. It is equally important to avoid subsuming many of the canons of analytic technique into forms of playing, no matter how intriguing the project.

As psychoanalysis has grown and developed both clinically and theoretically, more and more analysts influenced by the work of Winnicott and Bion, observe that playing and dreaming are not merely functions through which the unconscious reveals itself for analysis. Instead, many analysts discover that playing and dreaming are themselves part of the therapeutic process. We help patients to better play and dream in relation to their inner lives. Interpretation has become better understood as a kind of responsiveness to the patient's associations, a responsiveness that helps patients to play or dream, permitting a greater understanding of what they have unconsciously communicated.

I believe that some of the most important functions of analysis involve developing our capacities to find expanded metaphorical and representational breadth of expression in relation to our inner lives. In my own experience as a patient and analyst, I feel that this greater capacity to play with our lot, including our relationship to others, is what best describes what we can accomplish in analysis. In other words, psychoanalysis helps us with who we are now, where we've been, and who we are becoming.

I see a connection between expanded capacities for playing or dreaming and Freud's comment that the goal of psychoanalysis is to transform human misery into ordinary human unhappiness. Self-reflection that emerges from good analytic work is itself a form of play about our own tendencies to repeat neurotic compromises or to try to work with trauma throughout our lives. Play often emerges as part of the compromise of good analytic work—to develop the capacity to find play in relation to psychic pain and loss. Play is itself, ironically, a part of mourning. While some of the ability to play with perfervid involvement diminishes as one ages, we hope that analysis will restore and develop some elements of psychic plasticity and playfulness. As I explore, the capacity to mourn is often para-doxically helpful to the capacity to play, just as the capacity to play is often a part of the mourning process.

At the most general level, this book explores how the concept of play figures into clinical and theoretical contemporary psychoanalysis. I wanted to set out on a project that made original contributions to understanding play in the analytic setting. In particular, I try to examine play in the context of transference-countertransference en-gagement and enactment and in helping patients to develop capacities for symbolization and mourning in the analytic process.

The book emerged from two keynote lectures in 2018 (Cooper, 2018, 2019) one for the American Psychoanalytic Association and the other for the Centenary of the *International Journal of Psychoanalysis*. These papers developed ways of conceptualizing play in helping patients to move from unrepresented to more symbolized forms of experience. Each paper began to introduce a theme that I develop through a number of clinical examples. Specifically, I examine the relationship between play and transference-countertransference enactment. Playing often occurs in relation to the internalized objects of both patient and analyst, arriving to help find ways to better understand transference-countertransference entanglements. I elaborate ways that play as metacommunication (e.g. Benjamin, 2016) adding recognition while maintaining necessary paradox between what is inside/outside and real/not real (see also, Pizer, 1996).

I consider a few essential questions about psychoanalysis in the last 50 years: How do we reach our patient whose capacities for symbolization and metaphor are highly limited or undeveloped? How does our patient make use of us when the most profound experience she has of us is absence and loss? How do we think about play in the context of parental absence? How do we translate the syntax of visceral experience into deeper levels of semantic meaning, those that play seeks to facilitate? How do we survive repetition and deadness in order to become an alive subject and usable object to our patient? How do we facilitate mourning through play? Given the risks that play incurs, how might we develop what I call "an ethic of play"? Any attempt to examine an ethic of play involves understanding better the tensions between immersion, interaction, and stepping back (e.g. Civitarese, 2008b).

In each chapter, I explore how we, as analysts, change and struggle to change as subjects, if patients are to be able to make use of us as objects during play. Winnicott uses the term "destruction" in his paper on the Use of the Object in many different ways. He refers to the destruction of omnipotent fantasies as well as attacks on the analyst as an actual object. I will translate the meaning of these constructs as I have learned about them in reference to patients who struggle with symbolization.

Throughout the book, I try to develop some of Winnicott's most important ideas about play and meld them with the analyst's subjective participation in the therapeutic process. Numerous authors in the last 20 years have also done so (e.g. Benjamin, 1988; Bromberg, 1996; Cooper, 2018, 2019; Fabozzi, 2016; Ogden 2016; Parsons, 1999; Pizer, 1996; Ringstrom, 2001). In this book, I elaborate on the analyst's role as participant in and guardian of play, guided by Winnicott's concept of the use of the object. One of the challenges of describing play within transference-countertransference engagement is that play issues from the very intersubjective engagement that it seeks to interrogate.

I explore how the setting of psychoanalysis mobilizes play between patient and analyst. Particular qualities of the setting, including opportunities for free association, intimacy, and limit, facilitate necessary illusions for analytic work to occur. As a symbolizing situation, analysis translates unconscious conflict and fantasy, using what unfolds in the transference to create meaning. As we know, in the context of parental absence, often our work sparks the patient's awareness of the absence of others who were unable to metabolize their experience. These patients are disbelievers about us as transformational objects and often make little distinction between material and psychic reality. Part of what I believe Winnicott refers to as destruction for these patients relates to their unconscious attempts to destroy the symbolizing work of the analysis and the working of the analyst's mind. It is rarely useful to interpret the patient's unconscious effort to destroy the setting of analysis because it is an incomprehensible language of analytic formulation. Instead, it is better over time to find the patient's often obscure rules of play. We have to find their own internalized setting (Parsons, 2006) for their ways of feeling and not feeling that collides with the symbolizing activity and values of psychoanalysis.

I develop the ways that limit is partly constitutive of play in the analytic setting, an idea that was a vital part of Winnicott's theory of play but has been given less attention than the elements of holding and containment. In a chapter entitled "The Limits of Intimacy and the Intimacy of Limit: Play and Its Relation to Internal Objects," I examine how play is often organized around tensions between limit and possibility. There is much play in psychoanalysis related to the tensions between erotic experience/transference and the limits and constraints of the analytic situation. Play emerges quite often from the analyst's experience of limit in the countertransference. Often the limits of patient and analyst are related to how much patient and analyst can bear with regard to sadness, anger, longing, desire, and excitement. These limits have tremendous possibility for generating growth and understanding. This work was introduced in Winnicott's seminal paper on The Use of the Object in which he saw a generative, creative possibility for "destructiveness."

An important manifestation of play in clinical work involves what I refer to as "the play of mourning." Through play, the patient's attachment to an internal object as enacted in transference-countertransference engagement is slowly replaced with an ability to observe the internal object in a different developmental context than that which originally gave rise to it. The patient can observe this internalized object as a debilitating type of psychic forfeit, often in a new way within the transference-countertransference context of analysis. One of the chapters in the book looks at two clinical examples and a poem by Elizabeth Bishop, "One Art," in order to develop the relationship of play to mourning.

In one chapter in particular, "I Want You to Be: Thinking about Interpretation in Winnicott's Ontological Psychoanalysis," and as a current throughout the book, I examine Winnicott's unique view of interpretation and his invention (along with Bion) of ontological psychoanalysis. Ogden (2019) has powerfully linked Winnicott and Bion as creating a new way of thinking about analysis through their focus on playing and dreaming. As Ogden (2019) detailed, the distinctions between the epistemological (Freud/Klein) and ontological (Winnicott/Bion) are important to draw, though of course they are often linked. Winnicott was as interested in helping patients to be with themselves as to know themselves. I try to explore how the dimensions of knowing and being often emerge in different parts of analytic process, even with the same patient.

There are many interesting and unique qualities of Winnicott's view of interpretation that influenced psychoanalysis. We are still integrating his views of interpretation and making use of his ideas in various applications of clinical psychoanalysis. In the main chapter examining Winnicott's ontological analysis, I take up some of Hannah Arendt's (1996) views on love, defined by her and St. Augustine as: "I want you to be." I consider how this understanding of love intersects with helping patients to become more themselves through therapeutic work, particularly when patients coming for analysis want to change some of their "ways of being."

In the final chapter, I explore how the original work of Stephen Mitchell's (1984) critique of the developmental tilt hypothesis, brilliant and important as it was, did not take up the most unique qualities of Winnicott's revolutionary contributions to psychoanalytic play. While Mitchell offered a critique of most object relations theorists for attributing the development of object relations and relational processes to the earliest parts of life, he did not fully take into account the ways that Winnicott uniquely described various relational processes as occurring through the life cycle.

For Winnicott, we are never really fully able to parse what is inside and outside. Instead we struggle throughout life to work and play in this ambiguity. In fact, Winnicott's theory of play as a dyadic and intersubjective phenomenon never fit well into Mitchell's developmental tilt hypothesis. Mitchell focused on the regressive emphasis of most of the object relations theorists rather than the symmetrical elements of play between patient and therapist that were points of focus for Winnicott. This is important because I believe that the independent tradition in the United Kingdom and the interpersonal/relational traditions in the United States have always had some important areas of overlap and share Ferenczi as a common ancestor.

Finally, throughout this book, I explore what I refer to as an ethic of play. For therapists who regard play as central to the therapeutic action of psychotherapeutic work, what are the guardrails to help us distinguish between playing with the patient versus "playing the patient"? Is play intrinsically seductive? If so, how does the analyst maintain an awareness of the potential or even likelihood of transference-countertransference enactment?

One of the things that activates and enlivens play is the risk and uncertainty about where things will go. Play is partly defined by the idea that rules are always changing and being reinvented in play. How do we reconcile those laws of play with the fixed and important dimensions of safety and limit in the analytic setting? How do we integrate the transit of play with the stability and trust of patient and analyst? Playing is less an achievement in analytic work than a process that evolves and is its own reward, a process to live by and be in. In our work, we try to grab hold of these processes for a moment in order to speak with each other about what we do in psychoanalysis.

References

Arendt, H. (1996) *Love and Saint Augustine*, ed. Joanna Vecchiarelli Scott and Judith Chelius Stark. Chicago: The University of Chicago Press.

Benjamin, J. (1988) *The Bonds of Love: Psychoanalysis, Feminism, and the Problem of Domination*. New York: Pantheon Books.

Benjamin, J. (2016) From enactment to play: Metacommunication, acknowledgement, and the third of paradox. *Rivista Di Psicoanalisi*. 62: 565–593.

Bromberg, P. M. (1996) *Standing in the Spaces: Essays on Clinical Process, Trauma and Dissociation*. Hillsdale, NJ: The Analytic Press.

Civitarese, G. (2008a) *The Intimate Room: Theory and Technique of the Analytic Field*. London: Routledge.

Civitarese, G. (2008b) Immersion versus interactivity and the analytic field. *Int. J. Psychoanal*. 89: 209–230.

Cooper, S. H. (2018) Playing in the darkness: Use of the object and use of the subject. *J. Amer. Psychoanal. Assn*. 66(4): 743–765.

Cooper, S. H. (2019) A theory of the setting: The transformation of unrepresented experience and play. *Int. J. Psycho-Anal*. 100: 1439–1454.

Cooper, S. H. (2021) Toward an ethic of play. *Psychanalytic Q*. 90(3): 373–397.

D'Angour, A. (2013) Plato and play. *American Journal of Play*. 5: 293–317.

Erikson, E. (1950) *Childhood and Society*. New York: Norton & Company.

Fabozzi, P. (2016) The use of the analyst and the sense of being real: The clinical meaning of Winnicott's "The Use of an Object". *Psychoanal Q*. 85(1): 1–34.

Fairbairn, R. (1958) On the nature and aims of psychoanalytical treatment. *Int. J. Psycho-Anal*. 39: 374–385.

Ferenczi, S. (2013) *Sex in Psychoanalysis*. London: Read Books Ltd.

Freud, S. (1914) Remembering, repeating, and working through. *S.E*. 12: 145–156.

Huizinga, J. (1932) *Homo Ludens: A Study of the Play Element in Culture*. New York: Beacon Press.

Johnson, S. (2016) *Wonderland: How Play Made the Modern World*. New York: Riverhead Books.

Mitchell, S. (1984) Object relations theories and the developmental tilt. *Contemp. Psychoanal*. 20: 473–499.

Ogden, T. H. (2016) Destruction reconceived: On Winnicott's 'The Use of an Object and Relating through Identifications.' *Int. J. Psycho-Anal*. 97(5): 1243–1262.

Ogden, T. H. (2019) Ontological psychoanalysis or "What do you want to be when you grow up?" *Psycho. Q*. 88: 661–684.

Parsons, M. (1999) The logic of play in psychoanalysis. *Int. J. Psycho-Anal*. 80(5): 871–884.

Parsons, M. (2006) The analyst's countertransference to the analytic process. *Int. J. Psychoanal*. 87: 1183–1198.

Pizer, S. A. (1996) The negotiation of paradox in the analytic process. *Psychoanal. Dial.* 2: 215–240.

Plato. (1997) *Collected Works.* Indianapolis/Cambridge: Hackett Publishing Company.

Ringstrom, P. A. (2001) Cultivating the improvisational in psychoanalytic treatment. *Psychoanal. Dial.* 11(5): 727–754.

Rosenfeld, H. (1987) *Impasse and Interpretation: Therapeutic Action in the Psychoanlaytic Treatment of Psychotic, Borderline, and Neurotic Patients.* London: New Library of Psychoanalysis.

Roussilon, R. (2011) *Primitive Agony and Symbolization.* London: Karnac.

Stern, D. (1990) Courting surprise: Unbidden perceptions in clinical practice. *Contemp. Psychoanal.* 56: 452–478.

Stern, D. (2015) *Relational Freedom: Emergent Properties of the Interpersonal Field.* New York: Routledge.

Winnicott, D. W. (1968a) Playing: Its theoretical status in the clinical situation. *Int. J. Psycho-Anal.* 49: 591–599.

Winnicott, D. W. (1968b) The place where we live. *The Collected Works of D.W. Winnicott, ed. L. Caldwell and H.T. Robinson.* 58: 221–227.

Chapter 1

Playing in the Darkness: Use of the Object and Use of the Subject [1]

Consider a few essential questions that have emerged in the last 50 years of psychoanalytic practice and theory. How do we reach our patient whose capacities for symbolization and metaphor are highly limited or undeveloped? How does our patient make use of us when the most profound experience she has of us is absence and loss? How do we think about play in the context of absence? How do we translate the syntax of visceral experience when our patient finds us repeatedly speaking a foreign language? And how do we survive repetition and deadness in order to become an alive and usable person with our patient?

In this chapter, I aim to take us, clinically and theoretically, inside a process that I will refer to as playing in the darkness. This play occurs often with patients who have experienced no small measure of parental absence and who have lacunae in the area of symbolization. This play occurs eerily in what Henri Rey (1988, p. 461) termed "ambulant cemeteries," where loss is ubiquitous, little is easily decipherable, and sight lines, horizons, and vistas blur.

Introduction

I will interweave three basic currents in this chapter. The primary purpose of the chapter is clinical. I consider patients for whom symbolization is selectively undeveloped or compromised and who have often experienced a great deal of parental absence, neglect, and loss. I distinguish absence from what we refer to in the literature as "the dead mother syndrome" (Green, 1986). The dead mother syndrome involves an even higher degree of concentrated parental loss or intergenerational loss.

DOI: 10.4324/9781003265078-2

For some of these patients, the very setting and function of analysis as a symbolizing situation collides with and overwhelms the patient's capacity for reflection and play. At particular inflexion points it is sometimes possible to find the patient's obscure rules of play and fantasy permitting translation of unconscious experience into meaningful metaphor. These rules of play are obscure because they are covered over and defended against by the patient and sometimes inaccessible to the analyst as well. The rules of play are invented out of early contexts involving loss, overstimulation, and unconscious conflict and the circumstances that help create private rules of play are only revealed over time. Patients who have experienced a great deal of parental absence have more trouble finding play that helps to mitigate loss, such as fort da. We find that often play occurs at transitions between, in Bleger's (1967a, b) terms, "process" and "non-process," or represented versus unrepresented experiences, in the analytic setting (Cooper, in press). In other words, play and its accompanying rules emerge when previously unseen psychic possibilities for integrating feelings and ideas come into consciousness.

Secondly, I interrogate how Freud and Winnicott explored play as it relates to psychoanalytic work. Freud's play exists in the hide and seek and peek a boo of unconscious life. For Freud (1908), the opposite of play is not what is serious but what is real. And finally, Freud's play is revealed in his scandalous and subversive assertion to each of us: "You are not quite who you think that you are or were." I will deconstruct Freud's embedded subjectivity in the paradoxical elements of classic interpretation—indeed, in all forms of interpretation.

Winnicott understood that one can only have traction in exploring Freud's subversive proposition "that you are not quite who you think you are" within an intersubjective space. In that field we try to establish communication to repair troubled, often sequestered regions of the patient's internalized relations so that she might renew or launch new conversations within herself and with others. There are direct links between Winnicott's emphasis on play as what translates unconscious experience and Freud's (1914) groundbreaking observation that the unconscious must be enacted before it can be expressed. Winnicott's decision to feature play as central to therapeutic action was responsive to Freud's delineation of the vexing problems of how we go about translating unconscious experience into more conscious thoughts and experience.

The third current flows from my sense that in order for the patient to make use of the analyst as an object who will help the patient understand and better symbolize her inner experience, the analyst will inevitably change with his patient. Winnicott described the patient's transition from denying the object's existence as separate, to being able to make use of the object. Winnicott (1969) uses the term destruction in his chapter on "The Use of the Object" in many different ways. He refers to the destruction of omnipotent fantasies as well as attacks on the analyst as an actual object. Winnicott was always offering a tantalizing and exasperating ambiguity about what is inside and what is outside. He wanted us to feel how this could never be fully resolved. Ogden (2016) and, earlier, Bromberg (1998) have written about Winnicott's proposal that patients experience us being destroyed, which is often essential in the transition to being able to use us.

Building on Ogden (2016), I will explore my version of how we, as analysts, change and struggle to change as subjects, if patients are to be able to make use of us as objects. I will translate the meaning of these constructs as I have learned about them in reference to patients who struggle with symbolization. In exploring our countertransference reactions to being destroyed I focus on our resistance as analysts to this process of being alive and attuned to changing with patients who consciously and unconsciously object to our being alive with them. In doing so, I attempt to elaborate my own version of some of Ogden's (2016) rich exploration of how the analyst is destroyed and survives if patients are able to make use of the analyst.

Analysis, as a symbolizing situation, translates unconscious conflict and fantasy, using what unfolds in the transference to create meaning. As we know, in the context of parental absence, often our work sparks the patient's awareness of the absence of earlier others that were unable to metabolize their infantile and early experiences. These patients are disbelievers about us as transformational objects (Bollas, 1979) and often make little distinction between material and psychic reality. The light we try to shed is often unseen. Patients unconsciously negate the symbolizing work of the analysis and the working of the analyst's mind. It is rarely useful to interpret the patient's unconscious effort to destroy the setting of analysis because it is expressed in an incomprehensible language of analytic formulation. Instead, we have to find the patient's putative psychic reality, their hidden and sometimes undeveloped rules of play that collide with the symbolizing activity and values of psychoanalysis. Finding play is sometimes like a pop-up game in which previously unseen and unknown parts of the patient arise.

Often the patient's hidden rules of play are more visible in relation to the patient's experience of the analytic frame or their own "internal settings" for the frame. Play occurs at transitions between "process" and "non-process" (Bleger, 1967a, b) or represented and unrepresented (Scarfone, 2015) experiences in the analytic setting. Since the frame stands on the boundary between the unrepresented/somatic/sensory and the represented, I will argue that often play related to the setting occurs at the seam between the unrepresented and represented, and, in Winnicottian terms, allows for the transit from unrepresented to represented experience.

I tend to think less that there are dichotomies between the capacity and incapacity for symbolization and more that we all have various levels of capacity and compromise in this area of psychic function. Andre Green (1975) said that symbolization is always begun and never finished. I favor the notion that we are each, in our way, multiple selves with highly varied degrees of elaboration regarding sexuality, aggression, and capacities for love. Put another way, psychological integration itself is to some extent an epiphenomenal illusion and multiplicity of self and "simultaneity" (Ogden, 2004a) of states are more robust metaphors for understanding selfhood.

Patients involved in the process of negating or destroying the object/analyst and analysis as a symbolizing situation tend to have difficulties with attachment that take one of two forms. One form involves a search for connection that is fraught with terror of others and of the analyst as a separate person who will abandon them; object constancy is not "in play." There are others, like the patient I will describe today, that are more prone to degrade and "dismantle" objects (e.g. Meltzer, 1975), especially the analyst, in the face of depressive anxiety and loss. A bulwark between patient and analyst in the analytic field is often organized against desire and need; desire and need are partly represented and stimulated by the analyst and the setting of analysis. The patient is frightened to let his vulnerability see the light of day, akin to how precarious it is for archeologists to discover a buried village or town and realize that exposure to air or sunlight might destroy what had been preserved through centuries of darkness.

Often these two very different types of patients have in common a sense that their love destroys (Fairbairn, 1952). Parental absence is unconsciously construed as the child's fault. The patient is compelled to repeat and enact this dilemma by trying to negate or otherwise reject the analyst's transformation of the concretely experienced and enacted into feeling states and metaphor. Sometimes this includes hostility toward the analyst's existence as a separate mental entity. Our survival hopefully provides new play that defies their fantasy that they are toxic and destructive. In this process, the analyst experiences inevitable ambivalence about being destroyed, including feelings of guilt, inadequacy, helplessness or impatience about not being better able to organize affect, link thoughts, and convey meaning. If the analyst is to survive, he must also learn to find and deeply open himself to play that integrates the circuitry of his own internal objects and especially his resistance to understanding the patient's internal objects. The analyst must also deeply understand that a patient who has felt such absence both wants to be known but feels that she must remain isolated.

I suggest that at the heart of what we feel as analysts when we are being destroyed is a foundational ambiguity about whether the patient is engaged in protean capacities for play or whether the analyst is overlooking or submitting to more frankly entrenched sadomasochistic transference enactments. In a way, as we have to examine the patient's profound questions about playing versus being played, so must the analyst examine variations on this question within the countertransference in order to be of use to his patient. Mutual vulnerability must be established in order for deep play to take off, a point quite well developed by Benjamin (2016) as well as by Corbett (2017).

Consider that the verb playing has both benevolent and malignant meanings depending on context. Playing may either be creative, intimate, and fun, or it may involve exploitation, such as, "he or she was playing me." Playing and malignant pretense are like contiguous countries, and there is always the possibility of invasion by pretense into play's territory. This dangerous edge of playing is demonstrated in the use of the term "player" to describe someone who manipulates another in romance or in business such the playboy or the femme fatale. In the ambiguity of playing, we only find out with time who is playing us rather than playing with us. The nature of play is that it is often, alternatingly, both. In 1692, two girls in Salem playing a game of dripping candle wax on the floor to playfully forecast when they would get married was construed as witchcraft (Schiff, 2015). When someone was besieged by incurable illness and attacks by Native Americans, residents blamed girls, the symbolic mothers. The arc of this interactive mystery and ambiguity about whether patients who have been deeply disappointed by others feel that we are playing with them or that they are being played in analytic work is far-reaching.

I thought frequently about the matters of destruction, play, and survival with Sam, a young man in his late 20s who had returned for analysis, seven years after seeing me for two years of psychotherapy in high school. In our meetings during high school Sam was extremely reluctant to speak and our work had not been a setting for much levity. Sam's father had died due to an illness when he was eight years old and he was not able to get much of it into words. He had experienced his mother as anxious and preoccupied predating his father's illness. Now again in analysis, Sam wanted me to cease and desist from helping him see how sad and angry he felt and how much he never wanted to need anyone except in subterranean ways. Put another way, Sam and his feelings of vulnerability and tenderness were not really on speaking terms.

My affection for Sam was powerful and while it registered for him, there was no easy way that he could acknowledge it. I felt his appreciation and muted love that could also never be acknowledged. This was part of the darkness. During the roughly four week period of analysis a few years into our renewed work which I will explore later in this chapter, for the first time, Sam seemed to express more about needing others and me and hating needing others and me. He was developing deeper feelings for a woman than he had allowed himself before. At this time, Sam began a session in this way. "I had an idea that maybe I should come to our sessions, lie down on the couch as usual and you should leave." During this time, Sam often said to me as he lay down on the couch: "What are you still doing here? You still think that there's something happening here?" He would smile at these words and the first time that he said them to me we both burst out laughing. During this period Sam also said, after any comment that I made that seemed to matter to him, one or another variation on these words: "Time to leave" or "Our work is done."

There was no need to interpret his fear of loss, his fear of his own tenderness and the need to create distance from me as he was feeling—with his girlfriend and with me—that it was becoming safer to play. In addition to the usual attack on making meaning and translating affect, he was now proposing an alternative framework, one of his own fantasied choosing, and I was to submit to his mode of occupying the office.

Sam's laughter and words about our new analytic setting paradoxically include me in his pain by communicating his shame through feigned wonder about why I was still in my own office. Indeed, for perhaps the first time he was paradoxically recognizing that he was not entirely asking me to leave him alone; a new form of play involving a masquerade or hide and seek was emerging. It was also a new game of dominance and submission in terms of an obvious Oedipal uprising.

In Winnicott's dazzlingly rich statement of a particular developmental paradox, "that in order for the object to be created, it must be found," we could say that Sam was beginning to create his analysis by finding parts of himself and me. Finding was overwhelming. I must be dismissed. He was creating new rules because in play rules are always changing, often challenging and subverting previous rules.

Play often occurs in relationship to the setting. Time is owned and controlled by the patient. Sexual abstinence is abolished in the patient's fantasies and a new world order, a new set of ethical guidelines is put in place as a way for play to communicate unconscious fantasy. And it is also from the analyst's side that play, like analysis itself, is created.

Later I will explore some of Sam's dreams, his associations, and mine from this period that constituted some new kinds of play, dreaming, and symbolization. For now though, I want to emphasize that during the first few years of analysis, Sam's unrelenting disparagement of the analysis and of me expressed the danger of his desire and his fear of loss. Often my private thinking was concrete, my associations constricted. What Cassorla (2012) has called "non-dreaming" was apparent—still another kind of darkness. And internally, I felt as flat-footed as Sam frequently claimed I was. I could not find what Andre Green (1997) called "a ventilated space" in the absence that Sam was conveying. This ventilated space lies between the assertion that "this is meaningless" and the comparably reductionist other side, that "this means that." I often felt the way that destruction opposes play—destruction as the loss of the "as if" quality needed for holding in abeyance one's putative psychic reality.

During this most difficult period, my most optimistic interpretation was that Sam wanted me to be able to find sequestered, enigmatic, and disavowed parts of him that he could not say he wanted. I hoped that further play might emerge to reduce both his need to prosecute his case and to compulsively negate his longings; and I hoped that, interred in the creation of Sam's irreverent and subversive fantasied analytic setting, was a nascent capacity for grief and love.

Next, I turn to some theoretical undergirding related to play to help us think about the use of the object and the use of the subject in this kind of work.

Play as a Link between the Unsymbolized and Symbolized: Linking Freud and Winnicott

Freud's (1914) chapter, Remembering, Repeating and Working Through, introduced the concept of the Tummelplatz, the playground in between reality and fantasy, alternately translated as the battleground and hot bed. It is here where transference resides, and it is here where Freud observes that the transference is enacted before it can be remembered or expressed in words. Recall that this is the first time that Freud used the term "enact" and that it refers exclusively to the patient's and not the analyst's enactment. Freud was in a sense foreshadowing the subsequent new models of the unconscious, in which play, and the process of symbolization facilitate shaping the inaccessible past into proto experiences more accessible to consciousness and verbal understanding.

In the middle part of the twentieth century, along came Donald Winnicott, the principal cartographer of the development of object relations and of the psychic playground that lay in between reality and fantasy. In essence, when Winnicott (1971) tells us that the analytic situation is fundamentally one organized around play, he is bridging the gap between Freud's startling understanding of what cannot be expressed in words and what is actually being communicated. For Winnicott, play is what interprets and translates unconscious processes, including transference, for both patient and analyst in the analytic relationship.

The analyst according to Winnicott (1971) is both a participant and the supervisor of play in the analytic situation. Winnicott was typically evocative but ambiguous about what he meant by being a supervisor. To me the supervisory function means not only that we manage time and such but also that we are guardians who ensure that the analytic frame will be a preserve for illusion so that thoughts, feelings, fantasies, and transference can emerge as dreamlike. The analyst preserves and persistently translates material reality as expressions of psychic rather than factual reality.

Within this play, the rules of play are constantly in flux, being revealed to patient and analyst over time. Patience is required. As Civaterese (2008) and Frankel (2011) have suggested in different ways, play is a space for communication that is characterized by rules that constantly question themselves and each other. For Winnicott, we are *always* in transition from fantasy to reality and from inside to outside. What is inside and outside is never entirely resolved. We are always trying to play with reality. This *always in transition* has some overlap with Bion's (1962) notion that ideas affect and fantasy are in a constant state of expansion. And in much of my own writing, I have suggested that we are always in the process of experiencing and configuring what is old and new (Cooper, 2010).

For patients whose capacities for symbolization are selectively undeveloped, when things go well in this world of meaning the analyst is destroyed as an object that from the patient's point of view has required her to hide to begin with. We are asked (without being asked) to live in spaces for periods of time in which it is easy to consciously or unconsciously blame ourselves or our patients for not being able to develop shared metaphors in order to promote greater understanding. The analyst who survives destruction is required to work internally to better grasp how he may have resisted understanding the patient's need to be isolated, facilitating his survival as someone with whom the patient's experience can be felt and known. In other words, our resistance as subjects changes in ways that patients may feel.

Before I try to demonstrate how to find or facilitate play in this difficult context, consider that we are always embedded subjects in all kinds of interpretation. By using metaphor and describing symbolic meaning, by conveying forms of paradox and complexity in the patient's mind, the analyst is psychically touching the patient through play as subject and object. Interpretation's play is anti-illusionist in its immediacy and vibrancy, and practices discontinuity like music or poetry that involves us through stops and starts.

But for patients who lack this capacity for symbolization, interpretation is more like an offering from someone who is psychically alien. Play is not in play. Consider for a moment Freud's very familiar use of dense paradox and play in his droll and iconic statement from Studies in Hysteria (1988), that the goal of psychoanalysis is one of transforming neurotic misery into ordinary human unhappiness. While it is often reduced to an almost comical summation of how little to expect of psychoanalysis, think about Freud as an embedded subject when he makes this statement.

Freud's terse, monumental statement about the goal of psychoanalysis contains so many components of psychoanalytic play and paradox. He makes use of the agony and terror of misery (as an object), and juxtaposes it against something else that is painful but by comparison feels nearly light-hearted, ordinary unhappiness. Precision and succinctness is a part of the play. Paradox is by its nature self-critical since, like play, it is a process that is always questioning the rules that created its existence. Freud says that since conflict is ubiquitous, we are all subjected to it, subjects in relation to this fact of human existence. In psychoanalysis we have a dense concentration of paradox, humility, and the necessary fluidity between subjects and objects.

Going back to classical discourse, it was always important that the one who delivers the paradox be from the same economic, educational, or in this case, psychological class as those to whom he is speaking because he wishes to undermine or overthrow certain values. The receiver of the paradox must be able to experience the deliverer as enough like them to receive their words. A statement issued from the obvious asymmetry of analyst to patient, progenitor to student, or even, as some have suggested, colonialist to the primitive (Brickman, 2003), reveals a deeper structure here regarding a paradox of subject/object parity. Freud cannot say that psychoanalysis helps transform human misery into ordinary unhappiness without becoming a patient himself or being able to identify with his patient. He is both object and subject. Furthermore, our contemporary understanding of psychoanalytic work and play throws into focus the interpretive fallibility (Cooper, 1993) and subjectivity of the analyst as a source of understanding and resistance. Once again, the analyst is both object and subject, now a more fallible subject than during Freud's theory development. It is in the dense concentration of paradox, humility, self-questioning, and the necessary fluidity between subjects and objects that psychoanalysis thrives.

Freud shows that the interpretation that valorizes ordinary unhappiness sets the border of play, a border that consists in our compassion toward the patient's wish for something better than ordinary unhappiness. So paradox of this sort deals with itself as subject and object and plays back and forth across terminal and categorical boundaries—paradoxes play with human understanding, especially with rational discourse. Illusion and disillusion take turns, and in this respect, paradoxes might be called anti-rational. They are well suited for our psychoanalytic understanding of unconscious and irrational phenomena and psychic rather than material reality. They share respect and concern for the techniques they question, investigate, or challenge, such as the workings of the mind of the patient.

Freud is fundamentally saying that if the method that I invented is well founded, it is intended to bring into play mechanisms such as transference, that are governed by rules that are independent of my will. I too, therefore, like you, am subjected, am a subject in relation to these rules. In Winnicottian terms, I am a participant and supervisor in play, and like you, these rules treat me as an object. Similarly, when the Rat Man is asking Freud (1909) if he can avoid telling him about the torture that he learned about through the cruel captain at war, Freud empathically says to him that it is only through this method of association that we can help you. He states: "It is in the hands of God," which I believe is his acknowledgment that while he discovered the psychoanalytic method, we are all subject to its workings.

Put in still other terms, when Freud interpreted our wish that we could have more than ordinary unhappiness, in Winnicottian terms, he was destroying the object, the omnipotent fantasy that we could have more. What survives is a real object and object usage with ordinary unhappiness. Pretense that this will be easy has been laid bare.

What do we do to facilitate the process of play given the considerable constraints? What kind of mindful activity might bring the patient to the point of play? For Plato, the activity that best characterized play was the *leap* of childhood, an activity that Erikson also connected to play. Our various modes of leaping as analysts partly converge in Freud's free-floating attention, Bion's dreaming the patient and Winnicott's play. In the context of playing in the darkness, the analyst's responsibility is to be as attentive and curious about his psychic "leaps" as possible. Often it feels less like leaping and more like a slog. Most important are our attempts to eventually find or produce a fantasy or a kind of symbolization of meaning, one that is not a forced production from our patient's associations or our own. This kind of responsiveness is more related to our ability to give ourselves over to the process of play, to shape and shepherd it. Sometimes it involves our ability to be stimulated by the patient's unconscious fantasy when we are not yet aware of the existence or the nature of that fantasy (Beres and Arlow, 1974).

I especially like the way that Andre Green (1975) put it: "The real analytic object is neither on the patient's side nor on the analyst's side but in the meeting of these two communications in the potential space which lies between them" (p. 19). So, it is not only that we unveil a hidden meaning but that we construct a new, absent meaning, or a new kind of meeting created in analysis.

Yet I wish to emphasize that this activity, this disruptively constructive symbolization of meaning is precisely what the patient who has experienced absence needs to subvert or reflexively reject. This process of working with the patient's need to destroy and our survival requires that the analyst open himself to his resistance to this process. Ogden (2016) has suggested that we need to open ourselves to grasp "the resistant process that analysis needs to become in order for it to become analysis" (p. 1255). The threat of resistance to that state of mind by the analyst is constant and cannot be overthrown by fiat, good intentions, or theoretical allegiance. The solution instead is to welcome it without masochistically surrendering to it. I am trying to explore how much the analyst's attempts to know and experience his own thoughts and associations about being destroyed as well as his resistance to understand and resist being destroyed is likely to be experienced by the patient if she is to better understand herself and be known by her analyst.

The Incommunicado and Unsymbolized Experience

Twenty-five years ago, Robert Wallerstein and I crossed paths, each on our way to give discussions for two different panels at the American Psychoanalytic meetings, and he told me the following joke. From time to time the joke occurs to me in the context of this kind of clinical work, as it did in a moment I will later describe in my work with Sam.

Two psychoanalysts are giving discussions of a chapter. One was known for being loquacious, pretentious, and repetitive, while the other had a reputation for being succinct. After the chapter was presented, the first discussant spoke for 45 minutes, much of it repetitious and boring. Then the second succinct discussant arose, looked at the long-winded discussant and then the audience and said, "I too have nothing to say."

While there are many obvious interpretations of this joke or why I might include it here, I encourage you as you continue reading to consider an ambiguous, intermediate zone of play between the more accessible and saturated interpretations of the joke and several potentially evocative and ironic meanings that might emerge.

There is sometimes a shared space in which patient and analyst feel deeply the failures of symbolization. The patient's and analyst's cramped and fraught metaphor-building enacts the impoverishment accompanying the patient's experience of object absence. In this dimension, there is cynicism, often despair about whether there is even meaning to be found. Is the analysis a death march within the mind or against the mind itself? The unsymbolized is at best enigmatically represented and the unspoken takes center stage. Is the patient permanently isolated or is this in fact the intersubjective space to be discovered, the deep incommunicado that Winnicott spoke about in his remarkable chapter, Communicating and Not Communicating? For Winnicott, the incommunicado represents a key element of each person's vitality, one even more conspicuous for patients who have been badly hurt through early attachments.

We are required to understand that our patient may not be able to communicate or may not want to communicate parts of her experience despite potentially calamitous isolation. The more conscious decisions to not communicate are perhaps like John Cage's (1960) use of silence in music, a silence about which he said, "I've got nothing to say and I'm saying it" (p. 23). Winnicott spoke of "the urgent need to communicate and the still more urgent need not to be found" (p. 185). The other side of this dilemma: "It is a joy to be hidden but a disaster not to be found" (p. 185).

What matters clinically is how the analyst honors the patient's in-communicado since patients who have experienced absence may need to not be found at least for periods of time. The patient may need to experience the analyst's corresponding deep awareness that "I too have nothing useful to say right now" which doesn't mean being silent. It is a kind of abiding that Ogden (2004a) recognizes as follows: "it is not verbal interpretation but instead it involves us being that human place in which the patient is becoming whole." Or as Momigliano's (1999) recommends, it is an analytic attitude that is well described by "waiting to be, rather than wanting to know" (p. 39).

Return to Sam

Let's look briefly into the several weeks that preceded the moment in which Sam asks me to leave my office and the occasions when, feeling emotionally reached by his girlfriend and by me, he said that "our work is done." As I suggested at the beginning of this chapter, Sam and I had been involved in a long process of trying to understand his angry attachment toward his mother, his less consciously ambivalent loving feelings toward his lost father and his fended off attachment to me. His father died over a very brief period of a virulent cancer when Sam was eight years old. Sam, an only child, had felt that his father was a good and decent man and someone he felt was curious about him. The loss was also powerful because his mother was already prone to an anxiety that rendered her often absent and preoccupied since before his father's death. She had grown up dealing with her own mother's sense of loss of her mother (Sam's great-grandmother) in a WWII concentration camp. Sam felt, with some anger, that his mother's anxiety and loneliness always came first and that it was in his frequently requested company that she could feel more whole or present. In the way that loss trickles on through generations, Sam experienced his mother's grief for her own mother's preoccupation with maternal loss.

I had tried to show Sam many times how he attacked himself for his own feelings of passivity, need, and longing and at other times he attacked the objects of his affection, his girlfriends and me. For example, he would often experience his various girlfriends as sexually satisfying but devalue their personalities in one way or other. These attacks were "mounted" (a phrasing that I suggested to Sam) against depressive anxiety about his fear of attachment. He felt intense hostility toward his mother's attempts at caring, which he experienced as managerial and vacant. He was also still rejecting much that I said, particularly when it touched on the loss of his father and the obvious fact that he came to see me four times a week partly because he wanted much more than he could verbalize.

When Sam was not more frankly hostile, he was sometimes blisteringly funny in his critique of our work and of me, not unlike a kind of absurdist dramatist. He mocked his mother and me as hypocrites who covered up a kind of pretend parenting, paid caring, and management of him. His mockery also protected him from feeling abandoned because there was so little that was good to lose. In more playful moments, Sam, a man of similar height to me, frequently wondered if my good reputation was largely based on my height. While I could feel a level of hidden endearment in Sam's obvious contempt, I often experienced him as trying to disorganize me by subverting his and my own caring feelings, my faith in analysis, and my sense of responsibility for the setting of analysis and play. Despite my fondness for him and even, at times, a reluctant enjoyment of his dark humor, I struggled to not withdraw in the context of his angry rejection of what I offered. And he was correct that my offerings were at best meager. My imagination, like his, had often actually been quite constrained. For example, for years the only imagery that came to mind when I listened to Sam's complaints was the first Curious George story (Rey, 1941) in which George throws a great deal of pasta all over the kitchen walls of a restaurant.

As disheartening as these types of comments were, during the time I bring into focus here, I experienced Sam as slightly more playful and communicative than during his first few years of analytic work. Importantly, Sam had now been dating a woman for six months, someone he felt tenderly toward and seemed less prone to reflexively push away. He was even verbally amusing about his usual avoidance, hinting, I hoped, at an unconscious wish to be found?

For a few weeks prior to Sam asking me to leave the analysis while he stayed, he had had a series of dreams that focused on soap. The dreams were welcome; they were unusual for him to report, and in retrospect seemed to be part of the mild easing of his compulsive rejection of the analytic setting. In the soap dreams there was often a variation on my restroom being out of soap. Sometimes he was looking for soap, while in another we were in a locker room and talking about being out of soap. I had offered to him a few thoughts about how he might be trying to clean up messy feelings; or wash away the fact that he was falling in love with his girlfriend; or that he couldn't help himself sometimes from wanting to talk to me in the office or the locker room or to need things from me. Sam did not wash away these offerings with his usual dispatch, instead quietly agreeing, but still he did not seem deeply moved. Privately, I wondered if Sam was unconsciously experiencing me as or wishing for me to be a father with whom he could share the bathroom as a son.

During this time, I was more buoyed by the dreams and his playful inquiry as to why "I was still here." I was surprised though, that I had begun more freely internally associating to forms of dark humor, hostility, imagery, cartoons, and art that related to my sense of failure, anger, and a wish for revenge toward Sam. The joke of the two discussants was a regular visitor in my imagination, ending with the words, "I too have nothing to say." I kept returning to a few New Yorker cartoons, such as one in which the waiter at The Disillusionment Café states to his patrons, "Your order is not ready, nor will it ever be." I was realizing that "your order is not ready" was perhaps what had described our experience so far until Sam expressed his new creative version of the analytic setting.

It was as though I could become aware of feeling how for a very long time Sam had been unable to use me and I had been utterly unable to be of use to Sam and frustrated with us both. I had often had a fantasy of perhaps becoming the missing man, the lost father in the triadic relationship with his mother both as a paternal figure for him and to help comfort his anxious mother. But we were depriving waiters to each other (also in the sense of us each waiting for the other). I was a discussant with nothing to say and often he felt like a patient with nothing to say. Mostly I was becoming more aware of the degree to which I was sometimes silently blaming Sam for his inability to transform his catastrophe into words. My resistance to understanding how I could not be used as an object related to how, as a subject, I felt a sense of futility in finding the parts of his mind that remained hidden and incommunicado. I find it interesting that my hostile associations and ability to form imagery about absence emerged as I felt Sam relaxing and dreaming more in and out of his session as he conveyed his fantasies.

On the day that Sam told me to leave him alone, he half sat up from the couch, leaning on his elbows while still not looking at me and said, "I know what your stupid-ass mind is thinking about this soap stuff in my dreams. You are thinking about the old joke, "No Soap, Radio." I wasn't thinking of the joke on his mind but I was struck that his words and tone were intimate, familiar, and aggressively presumptuous. He had read about the joke in the sociological context of understanding groupthink. You may recall that "No soap radio" is a form of a practical joke in which the punch line has no relation to the body of the joke—that is, it is actually not funny. The participants in the prank (the joke requires a confederate) pretend otherwise. The effect is to either trick someone unfamiliar with the prank into laughing along as if he or she "gets it" and/or ridicule him or her for not understanding. Sam was beginning to better communicate and symbolize his mistrust through this fantasy. I said, "Maybe you think it's a mess to feel these things toward your girlfriend and me and it would be a joke to believe that analysis could clean up that kind of mess. They just don't make that kind of soap." He was quietly moved.

When Sam brought up his idea that I was thinking about "No soap, radio," I was not. However, once he brought it up, I had a whole set of associations to my sixth and seventh grade years when I recall the joke being told and the simultaneous warmth and cruelty of my close male friends playing jokes on one other—mostly taunts that challenged our masculinity, who was in the know about sex and power, and who was being left out of the Oedipal situation (the joke literally intends to make you feel left out). Sam's fantasy of my thinking about this joke reflected his efforts to play with his pain of exclusion and loss. The idea of a confederate for the joke captured something about Sam's continual enactment that I was not his partner in play. But he had been able to symbolize the betrayal and humiliation through his suggestion that I leave the analytic office while he stayed or through his fantasy about a joke that features my mockery of him or his of me. In an unconscious way, he had imagined me knowing about his sense of exclusion (with a welcoming mind) but had to negate it with my "stupid ass-mind." And through my hostile fantasies, evocations of the cartooned poetry of rejection, absence, and psychic "never," I realized that I was enacting a kind of betrayal or blame of him. My participation in this enactment and our shared dissociated actions (e.g. Benjamin, 2016) brought me into a stronger link to Sam's shame and hopelessness in which I was becoming or already had become a different kind of subject in analysis as an object for him.

Returning to this moment when in fact I was not thinking about the joke that Sam assumed I was, I had continually been thinking about the structure of the soap dreams. Sam was asking me for something, soap, something that would in his usual mode be humiliating and degrading as an action for him. I had several times, without remarking on it, been thinking about the Jews at concentration camps making lampshades and soap. As I reflected on it later and speculated to myself, his dreams convey his feeling that he was symbolically making soap for me through free association, not as a form of play but as a submissive effort to get his mother to know him. With regard to the ways that Sam and I are each making use of his symbol, Andre Green (1975) reminds us that the symbol is defined as an object, cut in two, constituting a sign of recognition when those who carry it can assemble the two pieces. This is fundamentally what happens in the analytic setting. The analyst often works hard to form a picture in his mind of the patient's mental functioning in an attempt to supply what is missing in the patient during the formation of "the real analytic object," an object that is neither on the patient's side nor on the analyst's side but in the meeting of these two communications.

In retrospect, I felt that Sam's fantasy of me leaving the analysis was a form of anger and play with his humiliation about the obvious but still unseen psychic reality that he was already more deeply communicating to me what had happened to him. My leaving the office would also correspond to his psychic reality of being left, only now he could feel more actively in control of the abandonment as in fort-da. And at the same time, I had somehow more directly collided (as a subject) with his experience of my absence for him (as an object) and how he wanted and didn't want me to leave him alone. He could better laugh about it. I believe that he is experiencing the analyst as a changing subject of play, or in Marian Milner's (1952) terms, a pliable object, and an object who could be better used. This is what I would add to our current descriptions of the analyst as a new object and our notions of internalizing objects. *A very large part of what we are internalizing of the analyst is not only who the analyst is but sometimes who the analyst is becoming or has become in relationship to the patient.*

We cannot know how Sam's and my insistent attempts to translate his affects led to his greater capacity to symbolize experience; nor can we know whether my silent symbolization, born of identification with Sam; my private retaliatory thoughts toward him; and my attempts to put something into words allowed for some of his movement, perhaps the kind of movement that helped him get some of this shit out. It seems to me like we were both getting some of this shit out. But I speculate that when I better located my own compromised ability to symbolize Sam's unconscious life, including my own frustration and helplessness with Sam that was becoming conscious, I had more viscerally and metaphorically entered into the bowels of his sense of degradation and anxiety about caring for those he loved. At this place of us each becoming more aware of our resistance to analysis being a resistant process (Ogden, 2016), subject and object are more blurred and sometimes, play emerges. And sometimes we are better able to see play that has already emerged.

It is also impossible for me to know the degree to which Sam could feel my sense of being destroyed. It is difficult for me to imagine that Sam didn't know and experience and bear the effect of his relentless criticism. I am in agreement with Ogden (2016) that one way or another, patients are able to sense their destruction of the analyst as well as the analyst's ability to survive destruction, when in fact the analyst is able to do so.

How Are We New in the Process of Play and Symbolization?

Since analysis is by definition a process that inspires resistance from both sides but also a process inspiring play with our resistance, I have suggested that in the analytic setting, patient and analyst are relentlessly, often quietly, repeatedly de-structuring each other, especially when we are trying to play in the darkness.

Historically, our theory of the analyst as a new object has been limited or inhibited by the understandable concern that this would imply manipulation of some kind, losing the frame of analysis, or that we would be minimizing the importance of repetition of old experience. Also, play in psychoanalysis is often so deeply intimate, creative, and so spontaneous that many of us who try to write likely feel that our best work is not something that we can easily capture in writing. I suspect that play is undertheorized because we symbolically and unconsciously equate deep play with sexual contact with patients—that no matter how symbolic the play, our work is exciting, involving, exhausting, and intimate in a way that is difficult and almost too private to capture in writing. It is often deeply and involving even when it is highly repetitive. The sarcastic phrase "get a room" comes to mind, which here suggests to me a psychoanalytic office with a patient trying his or her best and a well-functioning analyst trying to be as open as possible to his or her patient's fantastic inner life.

Poetry attempts to stop us in our tracks, to find the reader and challenge us to go beyond glancing at the page. Instead, when we read poetry, we are trying to play beyond well-trod patterns of thought and feeling. Poetry has the potential to surprise or unsettle us outside all of the real and virtual word and sound that seduces and surrounds us. As Wallace Stevens said about poetry: it is "a violence from within that protects us from violence without." Psychoanalysis also tries to stop us in our tracks of familiar, repetitive modes of minimizing, avoiding, exploring conflict. Stevens's comment is not far from Winnicott's (1969) and Benjamin's (2016) recognition that survival of destruction is predicated on the analyst's ability to get inside dissociated, wordless places of our patients to find new capacities for symbolization (Cooper, 2019).

The poetry, as it were, of many analysts through widely disparate theories, has tried to capture the playing mind of the patient and analyst searching for latent capacities for metaphor in the analytic field (Cooper, 2017). In doing so, we are Freud's and Klein's "finding" other (in the classical version of hide and seek and peek a boo regarding unconscious drives, motive, and unconscious phantasy); Bion's (1962) metabolizing and dreaming other; Winnicott's (1965) good enough partner in play; Kohut's (1966) seeing and mirroring other; Loewald's (1960) believing other who anticipates the patient's psychic future; Ogden's (2004b) intersubjective third that arises from the individual psyches of patient and analyst; Benjamin's (2004, 2016) moral third which results from processes of recognition, marking, and enactment leading up to play; Green's (1975) co-created analytic object; and Mitchell's (1995) other translating the permeability and movement between intrapsychic and interpersonal levels of psychic reality.

We hope that at some point our patients who have had to struggle so much in isolation may find one of these versions of otherness and newness while playing in the darkness with old objects and unformulated experience. I have tried to illustrate how the analyst's sometimes sluggishly associative and sometimes leaping mind, shimmering between understanding and resisting understanding helps the patient to better experience the analyst as an object, a changing subject, and a better partner in play.

Put another way, reprising both the succinct discussant as well as the well-intentioned bloviate one, we search with these patients for a foothold in a shared but often sequestered corner of intersubjective space—one in which, though we may have less to say than we wish, we must try to find a way to say it. Play requires from both patient and analyst a tolerance for inevitable and sustained uncertainty and sturdiness in trial and error. For the analyst it is aided by a "leap" of trust in our patients and ourselves.

Note

1 Sections of this chapter first appeared in the *Journal of the American Psychoanalytic Association* 66(4): 743–765.

References

Benjamin, J. (2004) Beyond doer and done to: An intersubjective view of thirdness. *Psychoanal. Q.* 73(1): 5–46.

Benjamin, J. (2016) From enactment to play: Metacommunication, acknowledgement, and the third of paradox. *Rivista di Psychoanalisi.* 62: 565–593.

Beres, D. and Arlow, J. A. (1974) Fantasy and identification in empathy. *Psychoanal. Q.* 43: 26–50.

Bion, W. R. (1962) The psycho-analytic study of thinking. *Int. J. Psycho-Anal.* 43: 306–310.

Bleger, J. (1967a) Psycho-analysis of the psycho-analytic frame. *Int. J. Psychoanal.* 48: 511–519.

Bleger, J. (1967b) *Symbiosis and Ambiguity: A Psychoanalytic Study.* London: New Library of Psychoanalysis.

Bollas, C. (1979) The transformational objet. *Int. J. Psycho-Anal.* 60: 97–107.

Brickman, C. (2003) *Aboriginal Populations in the Mind: Race and Primitivity in Psychoanalysis.* New York: Columbia University Press.

Bromberg, P. (1998) *Standing in the Spaces: Essays on Clinical Process, Trauma, and Dissociation.* New Jersey: Analytic Press.

Cage, J. (1961) *Silence.* Hartford: Wesleyan Press.

Cassorla, R. M. (2012) What happens before and after acute enactments? An exercise in clinical validation and the broadening of hypotheses. *Int. J. Psychoanal.* 93: 53–80.

Civaterese, G. (2008) *The Intimate Room. Theory and Technique of the Analytic Field.* London: Routledge.

Cooper, S. (1993) Interpretive fallibility and the psychoanalytic dialogue. *J. Amer. Psychoanal. Assn.* 41: 95–126.

Cooper, S. (2010) *A Disturbance in the Field: Essays in Transference-Countertransference.* London: Routledge.

Cooper, S. (2017) The analyst's "use" of theory or theories: The play of theory. *J. Amer. Psychoanal. Assn.* 65: 859–882.

Cooper, S. (2019) A theory of the setting: Play and the transformation of unrepresented experience. *Int. J. Psychoanal.* 100: 1439–1454. Plenary for centenary celebration of the *Int. J. Psychoanal.* October, 2018.

Corbett, K. (2017) Transit: Playing the other. Paper given at Psychology and the Other Conference, October 2017, Boston.

Fairbairn, R. D. (1952) *Psychoanalytic Studies of the Personality.* London: Routledge.

Frankel, J. (2011) The analytic state of consciousness as a form of play and transference. *Int. J. Psycho-Anal.* 92(6): 1411–1436.

Freud, S. (1908) Creative writers and day-dreaming. *S.E.* 9: 141–154.

Freud, S. (1909) Notes Upon a case of obsessional neurosis. *S.E.* 10:151–318.

Freud, S. (1914) Remembering, repeating, and working through (further recommendations on the technique of psychoanalysis). *S.E.* 12: 145–156.

Freud, S. and Breuer, J. (1888) *Studies in hysteria. S.E.* 2:1–323.

Green, A. (1975) The analyst, symbolization, and absence in the analytic setting (on changes in analytic practice and analytic experience) – in memory of D. W. Winnicott. *Int. J. Psych-Anal.* 56: 9–22.

Green, A. (1986) 'The dead mother'. In: *On Private Madness* (pp. 142–173). London: Hogarth Press. Translated by Katherine Aubertin from 'La mère morte', *Narcissisme de vie, narcissisme de mort*, Éditions de Minuit, 1983.

Green, A. (1997) The intuition of the negative in playing and reality. *Int. J. Psycho-Anal.* 78: 1071–1084.

Kohut, H. (1966) Forms and transformations of narcissism. *J. Amer. Psychoanal. Assn.* 14: 243–272.

Loewald, H. (1960) On the therapeutic action of psycho-analysis. *Int. J. Psychoanal.* 41: 16–33.

Meltzer, D. (1975) *Explorations in Autism: A Psychoanalytic Study.* Perthsire: Clunie Press.

Milner, M. (1952) Aspects of symbolism is comprehension of the not-self. *Int. J. Psychoanal.* 33: 181–195.

Mitchell, S. A. (1995). Interaction in the Kleinian and interpersonal traditions. *Contemp. Psychoanal.* 31: 65.

Momagliano, L. (1992) *Shared Experience: The Psychoanalytic Dialogue.* London: Karnac Press.

Ogden, T. (1989) On the concept of an autistic-contiguous position. *Int. J. Psychoanal.* 70: 127–140.

Ogden, T. (1991) Analyzing the matrix of transference. *Int. J. Psychoanal.* 72: 593–605.

Ogden, T. (1994) *Subjects of Analysis.* London: Karnac.

Ogden, T. (2004a) On holding and containing, being and dreaming. *Int. J. Psychoanal.* 85(6): 1349–1364.

Ogden, T. (2004b) The analytic third: Implications for psychoanalytic theory and technique. *Psychoanal. Q.* 73: 167–195.

Ogden, T. (2016) Destruction reconceived: On Winnicott's 'The Use of an Object and Relating through Identifications'. *Int. J. Psycho-Anal.* 97(5): 1243–1262.

Rey, H. A. (1941) *Curious George.* New York: Houghton Mufflin Company.

Rey, H. (1988) What do patients bring to analysis. *Int. J. Psychoanal.* 69: 459–470.

Scarfone (2015) *The Unpast: The Actual Unconscious.* New York: The Unconscious in Translation.

Schiff, S. (2015) *The Witches: Suspicion, Betrayal, and Hysteria in 1692 Salem.* New York: Little Brown.

Winnicott, D. (1956) Primary maternal preoccupation. In: *The Maturational Processes and the Facilitating Environment* (pp. 300–305). New York: International University Press.

Winnicott, D. W. (1963) Communicating and not communicating, leading to study of certain opposites. In: *The Maturational Processes and the Facilitating Environment* (pp. 443–446). New York: International University Press.

Winnicott, D. W. (1965) *Maturational Processes and the Facilitating Environment: Studies in the Theory of Emotional Development.* London: Hogarth Press.

Winnicott, D. W. (1969) The use of an object. *Int. J. Psycho-Anal.* 50: 711–716.

Winnicott, D. W. (1971) *Playing and Reality.* London: Tavistock Publications.

Chapter 2

Toward an Ethic of Play in Psychoanalysis[1]

Playing is one of the most difficult phenomena to define in psycho-analytic work. Winnicott (1968a, b) offered several general defini-tions, assiduously avoiding being overly detailed and specific in any of them. At one level of theoretical discourse, play can be seen as the underlying logic that makes psychoanalysis possible (e.g. Parsons, 1999). There are also particular forms of responsiveness between patient and analyst, referred to as playing, that involve specific forms of transference-countertransference engagement.

Winnicott (1968a) described the operation of play in a general way as follows:

> Psychotherapy takes place in the overlap of two areas of playing, that of the patient and that of the therapist. Psychotherapy has to do with two people playing together. The corollary of this is that where playing is not possible then the work done by the therapist is directed toward bringing the patient from a state of not being able to play into a state of being able to play.

Contrast this general remark with something closer to a definition in the same paper (Winnicott, 1968a, p. 308).

The thing about playing is always the precariousness of the inter-play of personal psychic reality and the experience of control of objects. This is the precariousness of magic itself, magic that arises in intimacy, in a relationship that is being found to be reliable.

At this level, an element of play functions continuously to sustain and work with a paradoxical reality in which things are real and not

DOI: 10.4324/9781003265078-3

real at the same time. In this sense, play and transference overlap in that they each borrow from real and illusory elements of the analytic situation. Despite Winnicott's understanding of the centrality of play in therapeutic process, his definition of play remains general, not addressing how play addresses a specific element of transference-countertransference engagement and enactment.

In my view, playing involves a kind of responsiveness to each other, which allows new opportunities for viewing transference and defense, including the fixed rules of transference-countertransference enactment. I define playing as a process in which patient and analyst shift in the degree to which they are working from within the patient's unconscious fantasy, either finding humor or irony in the fantasy or more directly confronting the clash between internal fantasy and external reality. It often emerges in a different affective register or with a slightly new semantic basis from within the transference-countertransference, the very intersubjective engagement that it seeks to illuminate.

In my experience, play arises most frequently in the face of repetitive experiences with patients' defensive organizations that "lack something, and that something is the essential central element of creative original-ity" (Winnicott, 1968a, p. 152). Playing often arises as a seemingly spontaneous response by the analyst in the wake of long held colla-borations with these defensive organizations. Thus, playing is staged, as it were, from within defensive organizations. The analyst and patient have developed enough trust together for the analyst to respond in new ways, often more vigorously, to these defensive coverings.

Ringstrom (2001) in his brilliant work on cultivating the im-provisational was able to capture the patient's and analyst's efforts to find this element of experienced spontaneity, creative originality in Winnicottian terms. Ringstrom was describing an openness on the part of the analyst to find something original within himself in the context of stultifying repetition in the transference-countertransference.

I refer to these moments as "seemingly spontaneous" because what appears to be analytic spontaneity always arises out of a shared re-lational history and is itself a property of the intersubjective field. As Ringstrom (2001) and Hoffman (1998) demonstrated so clearly, analytic spontaneity can only exist in dialectical tension with more formal interpretation. However, spontaneity is itself a kind of shared illusion between patient and analyst. In the moments that I describe, the patient becomes aware that the analyst has entered more deeply into their unconscious fantasy or transference while there is growing trust within the patient and analyst in the ability to hold both the internal reality of transference and the external reality. I believe that even when analysts are using more formal or if you will prescribed techniques (which is hopefully not too much of the time), there are subtle shifts going on within the analyst that involve trying to find reverie, trying to find new forms of containment or patience and curiosity with what they are hearing. So the kinds of things that we call spontaneity for quite understandable reasons are often more conspicuous but not always more original than elements of quiet work going on under the surface.

This process, one that occurs incrementally over time, is another reason to question the common construct of spontaneity. The growing trust between patient and analyst that I will describe enables a greater interpenetration of the patient's mind, one in which we become better able to receive the sexual and aggressive experiences that characterize our patients' unconscious rules of engagement. In moments of play, patient and analyst became better able to creatively make use of the more rigidly held rules of transference-countertransference engagement in the service of understanding and love. For example, the patient feels greater trust as a result of the cycles including the expression of aggressive and sexual feelings that are met with the analyst's receptivity, responsiveness and non-retaliation. The analyst also feels greater trust in his own capacity or readiness to use his own aggression or desire that, in turn, helps to create the sense of spontaneity.

In this exploration of the ethical undergirding of play, I am interested in some questions that arise from this form of the analyst's responsiveness, which emerges from a deeper and more personal context of the analytic intersubjectivity that it is trying to help the patient integrate. Thus, the concept of playing involves particular ongoing requirements for the analyst. By saying this, I mean that there is an ethic embedded in play, one that is intrinsic to its function and meaning.

I will describe several difficult to reach patients with whom forms of play emerge from a history of more formal interpretations of transference and defense. In the moments that I describe, the analyst shifts toward a new balance of speaking from inside the patient's fantasy while representing elements of external reality. I try to explore the analyst's gradual process of entering more deeply inside the patient's fixed attachment to unconscious fantasy and internal objects. The analyst in these moments contains both sides of fantasy and reality in a special form of opposition where the analyst exists within both fantasy and reality, facilitating deeper affective contact with both. This position sometimes permits a shift into a different register where something new and creative can happen between patient and analyst. The most consistent shift that I have detected is that the analyst either enters more directly into the patient's unconscious fantasy or speaks more directly from outside the fantasy to the parts of the patient's experience within the fantasy.

Several authors from outside psychoanalysis have touched on the relationship between play and the development of ethics. Plato emphasized the importance of play in child development but proposed to regulate play toward a variety of social ends. Vygotsky (1934) was interested in how the play of children, especially dialogues both internal and with other children, naturally served the purpose of learning rules and integrating reality.

At the most basic level, the analyst's commitment to an ethic of play involves his commitment to reflect on whatever forms of play emerge from both patient and analyst. This commitment is naturally part of the analyst's general ethic of psychoanalytic process, but it is especially important since play intrinsically involves the ongoing creation of rules within a dyad and thus sometimes the revision of them. There is risk. As Winnicott (1971) described it, "playing is always liable to become frightening. Games and their organization must be looked at as part of an attempt to forestall the frightening aspect of playing" (p. 50). Often, it is only in retrospect that we can understand the impact of any of our forms of responsiveness to our patients.

Play only can emerge from within the shared ethical foundations of all of psychoanalysis, especially abstinence and a commitment to understanding. An ethic of play requires an openness to considering that forms of emergent responsiveness that seem to facilitate deepening of analytic process, such as humor, may involve previously unanalyzed libidinal and aggressive parts of transference-countertransference enactment. With regard to the use of humor, glibness on the part of the analyst is always a risk. Equally true is the possibility that avoiding this risk is another kind of transference-countertransference enactment, one in which a patient feels unmet in their own new forms of expressiveness.

Among the most important elements of the analyst's self-reflection is an ideal that play serves the purpose of deepening the understanding of the patient's unconscious life (Parsons, 1999). Play is serious business regardless of whether or not the accompanying affects may involve humor. While play in the form of humor or a turn of phrase may amplify the semantic meaning expressed by the patient, if the humor is glib or expressed simply for exhibitionistic reasons, it is likely not genuine play.

Far short of this circumstance though, it is usually over time that we can determine whether the conscious intent to use humor to deepen or amplify meaning serves that purpose or constitutes other forms of enactment or both. For example, some patients introduce humor or sarcasm as a way to express loving and hostile feelings that they are otherwise unable to put into a more direct language. This humor sometimes marks a burgeoning expression of these impulses even prior to the patient's ability to articulate these feelings within himself or with the analyst.

One could easily argue that an analyst conveying a joke may be "being playful." This is quite different than a view of playing as an intersubjective process that aims to illuminate elements of the transference-countertransference, the very intersubjective field from which it emanates. The litmus test of play, interpretation, humor, or any kind of responsiveness on the part of the analyst is whether it serves to facilitate the patient's experiential understanding of his unconscious mind.

The analyst's ethical position regarding play applies to both his conscious understanding of play as an underlying logic to the analytic situation and his unconscious participation in the analytic process. Consciously, the analyst often finds play at moments involving a shift in affective register toward what he is interpreting, whether it be transference, defense, or unconscious fantasy. I hope to illustrate some of these shifts in register through some clinical vignettes. The analyst is also committed to the axiomatic understanding that he will inevitably be engaged in transference-countertransference enactments if he is able to facilitate a deep and meaningful analytic process. This requires an openness to the daunting reality that all forms of our responsiveness may inadvertently impede understanding and growth.

Another part of the analyst's ethical position regarding play is to avoid too active an effort to find play. Doing so would involve an attempt to overpower an unconscious process with a conscious one, a valorization of memory and desire by the analyst. If it is partly the analyst's responsibility to "bring the patient to a point of play," (Winnicott, 1968a), an overly eager and ambitious translation of this mandate may truncate understanding. It violates a particular kind of ethical principle at the heart of play which is to be patiently open to the transference-countertransference and to keep working at understanding it. In fact, King (1979) described a necessary "passion" in waiting and the importance of avoiding premature interpretation. Part of being a "guardian" of play (Parsons, 1999) involves the analyst's watchful eye regarding his own need to be clever or to create pseudo-understanding of what is being communicated. Pizer (1992) has emphasized the analysts's responsibility to maintain potential space maximally open for the ongoing interplay of two subjectivities. Guardianship involves the management of the analytic setting and an understanding that the processes of self-reflection that I have mentioned are always ongoing, never resolved.

For Davies (1998) there is a kind of guardianship of play involved in the analyst's appreciation of holding in mind the patient's multiplicity of self-states. This was also the work of Bromberg (1996). Each author in their unique vernacular describe competing voices, conflictual self-states that are vying for attention. The analyst's guardianship of the setting then becomes holding and containing all of the patient's "bits and pieces" (Winnicott, 1968a) without mistaking one voice as the central, dominating actor.

Benjamin (2016) has written brilliantly on the complex position of the analyst in the context of the inevitability of enactments and the opportunities that these provide for repair. Enactments in her way of thinking allow the analyst through her felt and observed participation, including her self-reflection about forms of dissociation, to recognize and work with the affectively charged experiences of both patient and analyst. Sometimes these experiences may shift from what is initially incoherent, into greater coherence and organization. Guardianship of play here involves the ethical responsibility to bring me/not-me experiences of the patient into the room through re-cognitionand containment of what has been enacted.

The forms of responsiveness that I will explore are continuous with and linked to other modes of interpretation such as transference and defense interpretation, but they also involve a form of transit from something less affectively accessible to the analytic couple to more deeply experienced or perceptually observed (Cooper, 2019). Play is not accurately described as post-interpretive since it offers clear forms of interpretation. At the same time, play often evolves from earlier forms of transference and defense interpretation. This notion of how playing can evolve from other forms of interpretation leads to other questions. Do the forms of playing that I am highlighting sometimes emerge from various forms of countertransference frus-tration with the limitations of other modes of responsiveness to the patient? Do they sometimes create an unnecessary demand on the patient, or do they offer an opportunity to deepen the process, or both? The answers to these questions take place in the patient's ex-perience of the analyst's intentions, including their understanding of the analyst's ethical imagination.

Nowhere are these questions regarding the ethical foundation of play more relevant than in play involving erotic feelings, feelings of being cared for, and aggressive feelings. Patients experience the work that we as analysts are doing internally to be self-reflective about these various ethical guardrails. I believe that real play in psychoanalysis can only take place at points when there is enough trust and safety in the analytic pair to allow for a transformation of something that has been burdensome, often repetitive, and fraught. I will try to provide some examples of play in these areas and deconstruct some of what these examples might tell us about the search for an ethic of play.

William

This vignette features a young man's conscious and unconscious hos-tility and underlying sadness enacted in the transference-countertransference. I highlight some forms of play that developed from more formal interpretations and some considerations regarding the analyst's self-reflective participation in these forms of responsiveness.

William was a highly accomplished 28-year-old, single man who felt quite ignored by his father during his childhood and adolescence. His father was professionally successful but quite cutoff from others including his wife and two sons. William's father was moralistic and critical of nearly everyone he met. I had hypothesized that William's father's emotional distance toward his children and wife was a kind of compromise in which he titrated his contempt and temper tantrums toward his family but did so at the expense of engagement.

When there was a lull in our discourse, William would frequently assert: "You are not there." This experience was exacerbated when he started using the couch in our work about one year after we had begun. When we tried to look into this experience, William questioned whether there was anything to understand about it. I suggested to him, and he had already anticipated my thought, that this experience of my not being "there" might well reside in his old experiences with his father. William felt that I was falling back on his past experiences to justify my current behavior with him, my "silence." He was only partly aware that I was actually infrequently silent in our work. Naturally, I asked myself the same question that William posed to me, namely whether I was using my interpretation as a form of distancing in our relationship. In some ways, though, I felt that William had a part of his mind that agreed with my interpretation and that he was pushing us to understand something further about his anger.

As our work developed William noted some different feelings during moments of relative silence. William contributed that now, when I linked his sense of a past silent father with his current experience of me as unavailable, he began to sense me as more present. In an interesting turn, he said that he especially liked it because he now felt that he was able to imagine that he had provoked me into saying something and this outweighed whether what I had linked together was true. This reminded him of the ways that he could provoke his father's anger by saying or doing something that he knew would irritate him. He said, and I acknowledged as true, that it was one of the only ways that he could feel that his father was noticing him.

Now he was repeating a scene in which he could find a way in his mind to be seen by me when he worried that I was ignoring him. I conveyed to him that he worried he would have my attention only as a result of provocation rather than as something easily given to him.

In William's mind, this game of accusation, provocation, and response became more recognizable to him as a way to stage a feeling of not being seen. It had been a deadly game as well as a deadening one for us both. As he pointed out, "it's not even that I was abandoned; I was just never seen." The more this occurred I found myself able to address directly his wish to be seen and the hostile, sometimes retaliatory part of this repetition. When he felt a sense that I was not there, I could say more directly, "You don't know whether I am seeing you and not speaking, or simply not seeing." Gradually, William could psychically entertain these feelings for longer periods of time, yielding to something more spontaneous from him or me. And saying this to him earlier in our interactions, indeed led to fewer moments of silence.

William introduced into our interactions his fantasy of coercion via his father, partly real and partly his psychic framework for feeling that he could get his father to notice him. There was a set of rigidly held rules organized around hostility, abandonment and a kind of cruelty. Even as things improved and William shifted into a greater shared sense of how his past experiences were contributing to his transference experience, I was aware that, for me, these games had an unpleasant feeling of being actually coerced and had at times been mildly unpleasant. I became aware that William also wanted to punish me both as a neglectful internal object and analyst.

I also had a peculiar, humorous thought that in some ways William was only very selectively seeing me—humorous in that this is, more or less, a reasonable definition of transference. I was trying hard to listen to him and make sense of what he was saying. Perhaps this could be described as a form of projective identification in which he was unconsciously projecting his sense of being unseen. I felt unseen in this version of negative transference-countertransference. In the privacy of my own clinical imagination, I could understand a paradoxical reality in which I was upset that William had a transference to me, the very thing that psychoanalysis is organized around as a mode of therapeutic action.

William struggled to consider whether there were times that I was seeing him, even if he could not experience my seeing. I wondered with William whether he needed to stay attached to this form of dreadful play in which he had to instigate something that actually prevented him from feeling something new, namely that I was seeing him on my own without his intervention.

In what seemed at first glance like a kind of infinite regress, William said, "See, I've done it again. I've provoked you into saying something when I wanted you to." Then a silence ensued, and he spoke of feeling very sad. He knew that I was trying to be with him and listen, which he appreciated very much. I worried that he had felt anxious that he had destroyed me with his aggressive form of play in which he had to keep documenting his experience of not being seen with his father and striking back. This pattern was repeated in a number of sessions.

In fact, I believe that this greater capacity for feeling my presence with him had preceded these interchanges. There were already cracks in his fortress of insistence that he was alone. For many sessions, we had patterns of William's seemingly desultory interaction with me in which my interpretations were, as I put it to him, "manhandled." I meant that he incorporated what I said into his claims that he had to inspire me or irritate me in order to get me to speak.

William had to exert control over a man in his mind, a man he desperately needed to want to be with him. However, he was now better able to understand that I spoke to him when I had something to say and that sometimes, paradoxically, I had something to say to him even during our silences together (Cage, 1961; Winnicott, 1958). At one point, we even developed a vocabulary of categorizing those instances when he felt that he had provoked a response, but I disagreed. I termed it a "false positive." He found this humorous partly because I had entered into a vocabulary, really an idiom, that was meaningful to him in terms of his research background and his rigid way of dichotomously assessing my interpretations as simply correct or incorrect. More important, I felt as though he was gradually trusting me in considering that not all forms of responsiveness to him were a result of his nihilistic instigation.

William was able to shift in his analysis in a way that brought him to the parts of himself that engaged in forms of play in which he could punish rather than feel simply rejected. In these forms of play he was prosecuting a case against his father for his crimes of neglect and rejection. As William brought these experiences into the transference, he could allow elements of separation from these patterns and his father while having a new experience of me trying to stay with his angry, hostile retaliation. He could also gain greater separation from his omnipotent thinking that he could manipulatively eke out the paltry attention from his father that was there to get. Our fraught engagement, which yielded to gratitude and less disavowal of our intimacy with each other, sustained him in the sadness and grief he felt as he loosened the chains of his attachment to his father.

I believe that in the moments that I am describing, the analyst is able to better contain a new balance of fantasy and external reality. I was moving gradually further inside William's persecutory fantasy in which he is being hurt by or hurting his father while containing his anger and allowing him to feel a safer version of external reality. In the play that I describe, we are containing both sides, unconscious fantasy and external reality, in a special opposition that exists within and makes affective contact with both realities within the mind of the patient. This permits a shift into a different register where something new and hopefully creative can happen between patient and analyst.

Put another way, William and I were working with interpretations which were experienced paradoxically. When I interpreted in order to help him understand his anger, sadness, and mistrust, he felt at once that I was not genuinely giving to him since he also felt that he had manipulated me. William was gradually able to understand that in construing our interaction as something that he had provoked, he was renouncing the very thing that he wanted, namely my capacity to want to both know him and respond to him. He found ventilated spaces (Green, 1975) in his own near-perfect form of insulated, faithless play. In this faithless play, if he plays by my rules, he will be submitting to a world of being unseen. In this sense, I was working toward finding elements of play, originally introduced by William in the context of repetitive sadomasochistic enactment, that eventually helped him inch toward a greater capacity for grieving (See Chapter 4).

I also became more aware of his tendency to fall into patterns of instigating negative attention and was accordingly able to make interpretations earlier in our exchanges; this mitigated his compulsion to repeat these perverse forms of pulling me into his fantasy. It was only over time that he could understand just how attached he was to his sadomasochistic relationship with his father and with me. My holding and containment sustained him as he tried to disengage from this form of play and find new ways to take in my actual presence with him, less persecutory and abandoning, as a caring analyst. This holding was in some ways akin to Slochower's (1996) notion of "holding back" because by responding earlier, I was in some sense holding back an impulse to wait and listen longer to what might emerge. William became better able to be alone in my presence (Winnicott, 1958), a conclusion that I drew from his gradual ability to stop these patterns. William was able to feel sadder and eventually more appreciative of many elements of our relationship with one another. This ability to be alone in my presence marked what I would term a deepening of his understanding of these unconscious enactments with his father.

Regarding a consideration of an ethic that underlies play, I think that I was learning how to find William as we went along. As his analysis developed, I recall resisting frequent interpretations that formed in my mind about the ways that, through his behavior, he was preventing himself from feeling various experiences, including feelings of being unseen, neglected, and having to make himself a kind of "nuisance" (Winnicott, 1958, 1960a) in order to be noticed. At times I was aware at some level that I was falling into repetitive games of sorts with William, particularly when I knew that he would say, "I got you again. I made you finally say something." I was becoming more convinced that William was experiencing the hollowness of his interactions with me that were gradually yielding to his own feelings of sadness and the potential to mourn lost experience.

I believe that over time, William could sustain greater trust as a result of the cycles of aggression-met-with some of my receptivity and non-retaliation from *within the staging of his defensive organization*. Importantly, I also felt a greater trust in my own capacity or readiness to use the aggression. In these moments, the analyst experiences something relatively new and spontaneous.

Part of the ethical concerns of the analyst in the work that I have described involves the ambiguity with which we regularly toil as analysts. For example, I could not know whether more frequently repeated interpretations of the sadomasochistic enactments in our exchanges might have more quickly brought William to a greater sense of his need to grieve what had happened with his father. As I hope is clear, a great deal of my work in William's analysis occurred inside me rather than in my interpretations to him. I was seeking to find how William was recreating his omnipotent fantasies of controlling his father and trying to resist furthering his rough play through retaliating against him. Sometimes I could feel the wish to interpret to him partly as a form of retaliation in the face of his repeated provocative invitations. In other words, I was aware of a wish to "manhandle" him through my observations, not only to help him.

Nor could I know whether more frequent interpretations would have truncated William's gradual awareness of the empty and dull experience of his reflexive reversion to a nearly perverse game. A great deal of the ethical undergirding of play here involves the analyst's openness to the patient's ways of thinking in the form of a game that the analyst felt William was playing. This openness, or what McLaughlin (1987) referred to as an "expansion of data" regarding thinking about the transference, risks the possibility of an institutionalized form of sado-masochistic enactment within the analysis.

My internal work regarding the matter of the ethical foundation of play was to reflect on the positions that I felt cornered into by William in his psychic gambits. I was metabolizing a sense from him as a desperate little boy who felt unseen. He was playing a game and making up all of his own rules. I could also access a sense of being unseen by William, particularly in my considerable efforts to be present. Privately I experienced the humor accompanying my awareness that we as analysts are always only partially seen. I also felt that I was metabolizing his partly sadistic way of conceiving my presence as something that he instigated. He was always competing and taking the upper hand. I believe that in receiving what could be conceptualized as these protean forms of play, I provided a non-retaliatory holding, one that increasingly allowed him to feel his aloneness vis-à-vis his father and to begin to grieve.

Peter

Peter, a man in his mid-50s, had felt ashamed of his father, whom he viewed as racist, autocratic, and rigid in his political beliefs. Peter's father had died when Peter was 16 years old. Peter had remained ashamed of his father despite a previous psychotherapy in his 20s that he had appreciated and found helpful.

Despite Peter's considerable success as a father, husband, businessman and entrepreneur, in analysis Peter would often say things straight from the heart about how none of these things were true. He would say, "I don't know how to speak as a father or a husband; I don't know how to run a company; I am unable to give talks in front of my employees." By all measures his children had found him to be a good enough father, his wife enjoyed well enough their marriage of 30 years, and he was still the head of a successful company that he had formed. He both knew and didn't know that he was a sought-after public speaker.

Peter sought analysis because he had long known that he was psychically unable to hold the idea that he had accomplished all of these things and that he could very well do the things that he claimed he could not. Peter was familiar with interpretations that I made about how he felt that he unconsciously held on to his connection with his limited father, a father he loved, hated and felt ashamed of. He desperately wished for a father he could admire even if he had to obliterate whom he had become with the father he had. Peter seemed to appreciate my interpretations about his overriding need to stay attached to his father and how he turned against himself in order to preserve his relationship with his father. He would go to great lengths to disavow and destroy what was good in himself.

Despite his shame and anger at his father, Peter felt an attachment to him in a way that he could not trace to his earlier experiences with him. Peter's parents had divorced when he was eleven and he didn't feel that his father had been very thoughtful to his mother and siblings before or after the divorce. To some extent, though, Peter had a trace of feeling that his father would spend time with him when he was a little boy while his two younger siblings had more of his mother's attention.

Several years into his analysis, Peter and I were deeply engaged in his substantial disavowal of anything that was good about him. When Peter would tell me on his Monday session about a work speech that he had given on the Friday preceding the weekend, a book that he'd read, or something meaningful that he had helped one of his children with since the last time we'd met, he would say something like, "And how could such a thing happen?" He began saying this with a smile at one point in his sessions and after a while, I would occasionally mirror this sentence after he reported something good: "How could this be true?"

I had made a somewhat spontaneous shift into a different register of responsiveness to Peter. I was not aware of any feelings of hopelessness about Peter's treatment. This shift did not feel like a desperate form of responsiveness when other interpretations failed. In fact, it seemed to me that Peter worked hard and while his progress was not that apparent, I had a sense that we were working toward helping him. I felt that he had a strong positive transference, one in which he could rely on me. I was a bit surprised to join him in his destructive comments directed toward himself that were consciously offered as a form of humor and play. I asked myself, however, whether I was unconsciously identifying with his aggressive turn against himself?

Peter would often seem to feel almost a sense of empathy from me if he or I would say, "And how could such a thing be true?" He once said, "Empathy works in a strange way in our relationship." In this form of play, I believed over time that I could join him in a place of conflict between the good experiences he was having and his impression that this good was actually at odds with the psychic laws of nature instituted in his inner reality. Peter sometimes joked that these laws were akin to the law of gravity in the material world. In fact, we would sometimes laugh about not knowing that there were exceptions to the law of gravity.

Part of Peter's new relationship in the transference, one that I experienced as a deepening of our work together, was with someone who did not require him to suddenly renounce the father with whom he was desperately linked. By suggesting that feeling good would be a violation of natural laws rather than psychic ones, he could relieve himself of his responsibility in the matter. He didn't know how to let himself accept the things that he was. His subtle, ironic question, "How can this be true?" reflected how he was able to simultaneously, incrementally acknowledge his separateness from his father even as he held on to an unconscious fantasy that they would never be separate. Peter eventually began to mourn that the father he had wished for had never been and would never be except through inhabiting the reality of who Peter was trying to be as a father, husband, and person.

Once again, the case of Peter raises interesting issues related to the search for an ethic of play. While I felt strongly that Peter understood the emotional seam in which my comments resided, he could have easily felt that I was laughing at him rather than with him. In joining him, as it were, in his self-loathing and incredulity that there was no way that he could be a good man or even the man he was, there was a risk that his analysis could become a site of sadomasochistic enactment. For example, he could have experienced me as mocking him in the play, rather than accompanying him in his disavowal of what was good in him. It was possible that rather than perceive the play as a way to gain purchase on what was, in fact, good in him, he might have felt that I was simply joining him in his self-loathing.

Then there is the matter of whether my own focus on play here has any advantages over a more straightforward interpretive responsiveness. I had offered Peter many interpretations of how his self-loathing unconsciously preserved his attachment to his father. He could consciously be angry at and dislike his father while still being a loyal son through his self-reproach. Peter seemed to genuinely agree with these forms of understanding.

In retrospect, I believe that my joining with Peter's incredulity involved an unconscious enactment worth detailing. I speculate that when I was in my more conventional and customary interpretive mode, Peter's loving feelings toward me were more threatening to him regarding his psychic pact with his father. When I joined him in his humor, he felt less that he had to choose between us, allowing him a more incremental ability to separate from his internal object and unconscious fantasies associated with his father. I also joined Peter in his defensive glibness, in some sense allowing him to see me as residing more inside his defensive organization.

While play is often best understood as a form of protean understanding of one's unconscious life (e.g. Cooper, 2019), I think that in the case of Peter and William, the version of play I am describing here might be also thought of as a form of responsiveness that emerged in the wake of earlier, more formal interpretations. It is not to say that these earlier forms of interpretation can be positively deemed unsuccessful since that would be hard to parse as separate from the moments of responsiveness that I am describing here. With each patient, play emerged from an experience of the analyst in which it was difficult to reach a patient over time.

Nina

For patients who concretize their early longings through compulsive sexualization, an ethic of play is quite complex. One of the most refractory forms of concrete thinking involves patterns of erotic transference with the analyst that are also enacted through compulsively sexual behavior with others. Rigid transference-countertransference patterns regarding erotic transference are often the hallmark of early disappointments with others. These transferences feature a mechanical rather than erotic quality. One of the only forms of play can be found inside the depersonified nature of the patient's associations (e.g. Coen, 2005).

For several years, Nina's compulsive affairs with men and women threatened her marriage to her wife. She insisted with me in her analysis that she and I have sex since there was "nothing else that I could offer her in analysis that would be of help." I experienced these requests as partly hostile but even more as distanced, somewhat dissociated expressions of her depression, boredom, and hopelessness. I never felt as though Nina was particularly sexually attracted to me or that her transference had elements of a very specific, identifiable object transference. Still, I felt a bit pinned in by the request. She was at great remove from an awareness of a few things that I thought she was expressing. I felt that she wanted to know that someone wanted her, especially her parents. Through her affairs she was constantly trying to redress this grievance. I also thought that she was destroying what was available to her from those such as her wife and me who offered her closeness and actual caring.

I suspect that I also felt pinned by Nina's requests because she devalued so much of what I was actually offering by way of interpretation. I felt as though Nina was unconsciously playing an unpleasant game with me, one that she instituted in many of her relationships. The game began with the nihilistic declaration that there was nothing to get from any relationship other than sexual release. In trying to understand this with Nina as a way to cope with many longings to be seen and held, there was not much sense that she was taking in much of what I said. I was trying to take in her requests since it felt like one of the only ways to help her to feel safe.

Over time, I found myself becoming somewhat disconnected from Nina, almost fatigued by her emotional remove and occasional requests. This fatigue was the place from which a very different way of responding emerged, one in which I said something quite different to Nina.

At one point after many months of her dissociated, continuing suggestion to have sex and even more, her reflexive dismissals of my many attempts to understand what these requests might mean in terms of her inner life, I said, "I feel that you ask me that question so often but I am not at all sure whether you have asked it of yourself? Are you actually sure that you want to have sex?" Nina was stunned by my question and remained quiet for a moment before responding with some nervous laughter and then sadness: "I don't know." We continued from there and eventually I asked her about what she was aware of about herself when she would ask that question of me. Her uncertainty about the question remained for quite a few sessions, bringing her into a protean form of curiosity that had not been previously available.

In one sense this marked the beginning of Nina's analysis. Of course, her analysis had begun long before. To some extent, Nina had used the analytic setting as a place to feel held. She had also attacked the setting both in the relentlessness of her requests to have sex and the desultory manner in which she felt that there was nothing else to get from me but a sexual encounter. I think that it could be said that play occurred quite unwittingly, paradoxically, by a level of psychic penetration that Nina and I had previously found unimaginable. Maybe too, it was a form of intercourse that could be symbolized for the first time in analysis and in a way that mitigated some of her reflexive sexualization of her longings. Paradoxically, Nina could be alone in my presence (e.g. Winnicott, 1958) for one of the first times in her analysis even as she was allowing for us both to look more deeply inside her.

This form of responsiveness could easily be regarded as a defense interpretation of sorts, one that involved a kind of confrontation with her dissociation and compulsive sexualization of her longing to be seen. It could be translated as something along the lines of this question: "Nina, is the person who continually asks for sex a person you feel connected to right now?" Or, "Am I the person you want to have sex with or the person you so desperately want to feel loved and held by?"

I view our interaction through the lens of play in that the form my question took resided deeply inside elements of our transference-countertransference engagement, specifically from inside her defensive organization of externalization. In this moment, I was able to recognize and express myself in more active ways, standing slightly more outside a form of rigidly held transference-countertransference entanglement in which penetration had been concretized by Nina and by me too. In that bind, the question that I am turning back on her is one that she has not been able to be self-reflective about. I had found myself anxious that a more active inquiry into Nina's desires would be overstimulating to her or me. This moment suggests a loosening of our fixed transference-countertransference, one that is well characterized as play.

Regarding the analyst's ethic of play, I am quite certain that it would have been unimaginable for me to ask this of Nina earlier in our work. Perhaps another analyst, less worried about destabilizing her and less anxious himself, might have been able to more gently ask her the question that I asked. Despite the persistence of her wishes, Nina had worked in her treatment in such a way that eventually allowed me to say something that regarded her as enough of a separate person to be able to contemplate the question. It was a question that targeted in a new way, a new register what she wanted beneath her compulsive sexual behavior. Earlier, I would have been concerned that my inquiry would be interpreted as creating a hope that I would comply. I had arrived at a point where I could tolerate my own concrete fear of being swallowed up by Nina's needs to bump into me, have sex, and perhaps become fused with me. I believe that in retrospect I experienced something in Nina that could allow for such a question.

Obviously, the form of responsiveness could be seen as a form of seduction from my side. Is even the action of asking the question, "Are you certain that you want to have sex?" a form of seduction? Could the patient experience the question itself as affirming a reality that it would be possible to do so? In the universe of potential clinical contexts, I don't think that anyone can rule out a myriad of ways that such a question might be experienced. On the other hand, it is important to note that years had gone by in which I had little doubt in my own mind that Nina knew that physical touching would not occur in our relationship. In fact, my question to her was issued from a psychological place in which her anger and complaint about how unfulfilling her sexual acting out had been seemed much more prominent than anything related to her desire.

Regarding one of the more important measures of an ethical foundation of play, I believe that a kind of deepening was facilitated in this exchange. It was as though Nina could reach through my question in a way that had been previously inaccessible to her. She had been able to ask me if I wanted to have sex, but she had not been able to ask herself. In some sense we reached beyond the "empty states" that Lafarge (1989) described as a complex defensive organization concealing a number of other affects such as aggressively charged object relations and longings. It is in the mind of the analyst in which the guardrails, the patient's safety within the transference-countertransference and the analyst's, need to be considered. Similarly, the analyst tries to assess the impact of interaction with the patient regarding the crucial criterion of deepening.

In relation to Nina, what had been enacted was a kind of institutionalized dissociation in the analytic setting. I had felt pressured by Nina to an extent that left me unable to think and question my own mind and hers. I felt a degree of phobic dread regarding her question, likely a fear that words could be equated with sexual activity. My question to her was relatively unformulated but represented a kind of "analytic act of freedom" (Symington, 1983) which marked a particular kind of play within the transference-countertransference enactment. I believe that I had acquired greater trust in Nina to work with my question and perhaps a developing sense that our desire together could better coexist.

I believe that a degree of freedom to probe Nina's question promoted her capacity for self-reflection about a person inside her. We began to try better to speak to the parts of her that acted compulsively, pushing our inquiry into a deeper level of Nina's inner experience.

Discussion

A part of the analytic frame that exists in parallel to maintenance of the material elements of the setting involves the analyst's commitment to understanding forms of fantasy, behavior, and affect as communication about the patient's "internal setting" (Parsons, 1999, 2007). The analyst's necessary commitment to understanding the ubiquity of enactment means being alert to the fact that we are often retrospectively understanding communication. An ethic of play alerts us to the inevitable and constant emergence of enactments within the process since there is no way for play to exist outside transference-countertransference enactment.

In the context of risk that I have outlined, the analyst is required to consider that play may create a feeling in a patient that their defenses have been too abruptly removed or jolted, just as unwitting collaborative avoidance of these defensive coverings can contribute to stultification in the analytic process. Any version of play, more continuous than not with other forms of interpretive responsiveness, recognizes the sobering truth that we are always trying to integrate the rule-bound qualities of our adaptation to reality with the analytic relationship.

One of the most important guardrails regarding play involves the potential to side with the persecutory parts of the patient that can use analytic understandings as a further form of self-recrimination. The patient's self-effacing humor or the analyst's humor directed toward the patient can be turned against the patient in ways that are less noticeable than we might think. Here we are at the heart of distinctions between playing with/laughing with versus playing someone or laughing at someone.

For example, when I entered into Peter's incredulity about how it could be so that he could accomplish good things, there was a risk that he would feel criticized or unconsciously gratified by my joining him in his self-reproach. Play resided in his capacity to hold the paradox that his analyst would join him in his criticism, an attitude that he knew was patently at odds with what he had experienced with me. His experience of me over time is important here. I believe that often we find elements of play with patients that emerge from earlier forms of interpretation of transference, defense, and unconscious fantasy. More specifically, it is over time that patients develop the capacity to hold the analyst's role in their own unconscious fantasy while also representing new elements of a more integratable external reality. This may also be related to what Ogden (1994) meant when he suggested in reference to interpretive action, "An interpretation-in-action accrues its specific symbolic meaning from the experiential context of the analytic intersubjectivity in which it is generated" (p. 219).

I would daresay that in my shift into this form of affective resonance with Peter, I was "being" with him rather than more exclusively trying to understand him (Foehl, 2010; Ogden, 2019). I believe that Peter experienced me as more deeply understanding of him in this mode, but he was perhaps also unconsciously aware that I had, in a particular way, entered inside his unconscious fantasy. My question to Nina also marked a different kind of entry into her inner life, one that had been too difficult to do earlier in her analysis for fear of being too seductive or stimulating. I was able to eventually allow my own vulnerability, desire, and my own fear of desire, to enter into Nina's defensive organizations. In my view, this allowed her to ask herself questions about her own desire and longings that she had been previously unable to ask herself. The analyst's ability to better understand and contain his participation in the patient's unconscious experience in the transference while holding external reality is crucial to facilitating play.

We hope that under the best circumstances, the analyst has access to a kind of signal anxiety operating to help him see whether he is in danger of going too far regarding the patient's capacity to work with our responsiveness. When we are in dissociated states, avoiding entering more deeply into the patient's experience (e.g. elements of my work with Nina), we also have to ask questions about the problems presented by avoiding the kind of work that I am outlining. Mostly, this involves listening—as we do with all of our interpretations—to our patients to determine when we have truncated a process of exploration rather than expanded the patient's associations. However, we know that sometimes we cannot know in advance how our participation will be experienced. Some patients joke about their self-defeating behavior regarding their erotic or work life in ways that can mislead the analyst into thinking that these jokes reflect their self-awareness. Despite our training to the contrary, analysts can presume understanding and shy away from at least internally interrogating the meaning of these jokes. These instances reflect a form of pseudo-humor and it is usually a matter of time before the analyst becomes aware that he or she no longer finds the joke funny.

In some sense, we hope that our patients can make use of play in the same way that play is being used by the child in development to help integrate reality (Vygotsky, 1934). Yet there are never assurances that what we hope will help integrate understanding will not, instead, instigate a fear of the analyst and analysis as an unreliable holding environment.

An ethic of play always hinges on the reality that if rules in play are made up as the participants go along, both patient and analyst are also frequently shifting in their internal experiences of safety. One of the most important countertransference "activities" (Wilson, 2013) for the analyst in helping to bring patients to points of play resides in his or her ability to find ventilated spaces of our own in relation to transference-countertransference. This is another dimension of the ethic of play. It would have been unimaginable for me to say/ask what I said to Nina without being able to contain a myriad of feelings about her longings. In a Winnicott (1969) framework, I survived feeling both mildly assaulted by her sexual proposals and disconnected in my own distancing myself from this repetitive situation. I was able to tolerate my own desire and vulnerability in my work with Nina and became less focused on my defensive (externalized) protectiveness toward her. It is also quite likely that my eventual ability to experience Nina's demands as less concrete than I had earlier was a response to Nina gaining more ability to reflect on her compulsive fantasies. In this space, my countertransference was not bumping into her requests (e.g. Cooper, 2019; Ogden, 1989) as an attempt to locate the object (e.g. the autistic-contiguous position), but rather posing a question to her as a more developed person capable of self-reflection about what she wished for.

Wilson (2006, 2013) and Morris (2013) suggest that it is inherent in the ethical context of psychoanalysis that the analyst leave unadorned and unprotected both his desire and his lack. This capacity is always an ongoing activity on the part of the analyst. In this activity, if we are defining play as a form of responsiveness that emerges to illuminate elements of the fixed rules of transference-countertransference, there is an embedded understanding that this is not a process after which we say, "mission accomplished." Since it is fundamentally neither possible nor desirable to fully leave ourselves unadorned, we are always in a process of considering the different kinds of fault lines that I have tried to address.

The process of learning about the ethical dimensions of play is embedded in the general process of thinking about transference-countertransference as an activity. Returning to Wilson's (2006, 2013) notion that we are required to try to leave unadorned our desire and lack, the ethic that I have explored in this paper goes beyond the analyst's recognition of his own desire. In each of the examples I have described, patient and analyst are sometimes able to arrive at a new sense that the desires of analyst and patient can coexist and be held synergistically rather than exclusively in opposition with one another (e.g. Benjamin, 2004, 2016). These determinations highlight the constant adjustments that we make to our patients and they to us during the analytic process.

Note

1 Sections of this chapter first appeared in the *Psychoanalytic Quarterly* 90: 373–397.

References

Benjamin, J. (2004) Beyond doer and done to. An intersubjective view of thirdness. *Psychoanal. Q.* 73(1): 5–46.

Benjamin, J. (2016) From enactment to play: Metacommunication, acknowledgement, and the third of paradox. *Rivista Di Psicoanalisi* 62: 565–593.

Bromberg, P. M. (1996) *Standing in the Spaces: Essays on Clinical Process, Trauma and Dissociation*. Hillsdale, NJ: The Analytic Press.

Cage, J. (1961) *Silence*. Hartford: Wesleyan Press.

Coen, S. J. (2005) How to play with patients who would rather remain remote. *J. Amer. Psychoanal. Assn.* 53: 811–834.

Cooper, S. H. (2018) Playing in the darkness: Use of the object and use of the subject. *J. Amer. Psychoanal. Assn.* 66(4): 743–765.

Cooper, S. H. (2019) A theory of the setting: The transformation of unrepresented experience and play. *Int. J. Psycho-Anal.* 100: 1439–1454.

Davies, J. M. (1998) Multiple perspectives on multiplicity. *Psychoanal. Dial.* 8: 195–206.

Foehl, J. C. (2010) The play's the thing: The primacy of play and the persistence of pluralism in psychoanalysis. *Contemp. Psychoanal.* 46: 46–86.

Green, A. (1975) The analyst, symbolization, and absence in the analytic setting – in memory of D. W. Winnicott. *Int. J. Psycho-Anal.* 56: 9–22.

King, P. (1979) Affective responses of the analyst to the patient's communications. *Int. J. Psycho-Anal.* 59: 329–334.

Lafarge, L. (1989) Emptiness as defense in severe regressive states. *J. Amer. Psychoanal. Assn.* 37: 965–995.

McLaughlin, J. T. (1987) The play of transference: Some reflections on enactment in the psychoanalytic situation. *J. Amer. Psychoanal. Assn.* 35: 557–582.

Morris, H. (2013) The analyst's offer. *J. Amer. J. Psychoanal.* 64: 1173–1187.

Ogden, T. (2019) On the concept of the autisitic-contiguous position. *Int. J. Psycho-Anal.* 70: 127–140.

Ogden, T. (1994) The concept of interpretive action. *Psychoanal. Q.* 63: 2019–2245.

Parsons, M. (1999) The logic of play in psychoanalysis. *Int. J. Psycho-Anal.* 80(5): 871–884.

Parsons, M. (2006) The analyst's countertransference to the psychoanalytic process. *Int. J. Psychoanal.* 87: 1183–1198.

Parsons, M. (2007) Raiding the inarticulate: The internal analytic setting and listening beyond countertransference. 89: 662–682.

Pizer, S. A. (1992) The negotiation of paradox in the analytic process. *Psychoanal. Dial.* 2(2): 215–240.

Ringstrom, P. A. (2001) Cultivating the improvisational in psychoanalytic treatment. *Psychoana. Dial.* 11: 727–754.

Slochower, J. (1996) Holding and the Fate of the Analyst's Subjectivity. *Psychoanal. Dial.* 6(3): 323–353.

Symington, N. (1983) The analyst's act of freedom as agent of therapeutic change. *Int. Rev. Psychoanal.* 10: 283–291.

Vygotsky, L. (1934/2012) *Thought and Language.* Cambridge: MIT Press.

Wilson, M. (2006) "Nothing could be further from the truth": The role of lack in the analytic process. *J. Amer. Psychoanal. Assn.* 54(2): 397–421.

Wilson, M. (2013) Desire and responsibility: The ethics of countertransference experience. *Psychoanal. Q.* 82: 435–476.

Winnicott, D. W. (1958) The capacity to be alone. *Int. J. Psycho-Anal.* 39: 416–420.

Winnicott, D. W. (1960a) The theory of the parent-infant relationship. *Int. J. Psychoanal.* 41: 585–595.

Winnicott, D. W. (1968a) Playing: Its theoretical status in the clinical situation. *Int. J. Psycho-Anal.* 49: 591–599.

Winnicott, D. W. (1968b) Playing: Its theoretical status in the clinical situation. *Int. J. Psycho-Anal.* 49: 591–599.

Winnicott, D. W. (1969) The use of an object. *Int. J. Psycho-Anal.* 50:711–716.

Winnicott, D. W. (1971) *Playing and Reality.* London: Tavistock Books.

Chapter 3

The Limits of Intimacy and the Intimacy of Limits: Play and the Internal Bad Object

The powerful and refractory grip of our internalized "bad" objects has been one of the most persistent problems for psychoanalytic work. Some theories about the fate of the bad object suggest a kind of exorcism or "release" of it (e.g. Fairbairn, 1943, 1958) through analytic work. I don't favor the term "release," since it seems to turn a blind eye to how these objects nearly always endure as part of the internalized psychic economy of the individual. Does release mean loosened or entirely let go of? I prefer the idea that psychoanalysis promotes greater capacities to play internally and externally with our enduring experiences of others.

In a series of papers (Cooper, 2000, 2004, 2015, 2018; Cooper and Levit, 1998), I have suggested that our theories of therapeutic action have focused more exclusively on the experience of the analyst as a kind of new, good object (different than the historically similar transference object). These theories accurately turn our attention to the importance of factors such as the analyst's containment and an "inner attitude" (Nacht, 1963) of caring, respect, and the aim to understand inner life. For example, in a creative reading of Fairbairn's concept of "release," Ogden (2010) emphasized the "real" relationship with the analyst, including the analyst's deep acceptance of his patient, which, when paired with the working through of transferential elements, allowed a patient to relax his sense of punishing shame, self-loathing, and badness.

In this chapter, I emphasize the importance of benevolent elements of the analyst's limits containing transference and resistance in the therapeutic action of psychoanalysis. I will also explore how aspects

DOI: 10.4324/9781003265078-4

of limit intrinsic to the analytic setting (Cooper, 2019; Green, 1975) are used in play to change our relation to the bad object.

The patient and analyst's work with limits is complementary to the analyst's holding and containing function and is one of the most important functions of analysis. In psychoanalytic thinking about therapeutic action and technique, the analyst's forms of love—including containment, provision, and gratification—have been persistently split from the analyst's limits—manifested in forms of renunciation, abstinence and mourning. At a clinical level, play is what promotes the integration of these affects within the patient.

Psychoanalysis provides not only an opportunity to feel deeply understood and cared for but also one in which the patient has a new experience of the limitations of love, one that is substantially less toxic than some earlier experience. Sometimes the experience of limitation is based on the real limitations of the analyst that the patient has come to know and work with, while sometimes it may rest more substantially on the projection of the patient's earlier encounters with limitation and loss. At other times, the analyst's limitations in holding particular affects reflect an embedded interpretation about the degree to which the patient is defensively holding on to painful affect (e.g. Ogden, 2019). I agree with Wilson's (2006) assertion that the notion of lack is an integral part of the analytic attitude. Green (1975) also argued that the concept of limit is embedded in the analytic setting. Steiner (2006) and Cooper (2019) describe how elements of limit are inevitably enacted in the patient and analyst's relationship to the analytic setting. Finally, Wilson's (2013) discussion of the ethics of countertransference experience also implicitly relates the analyst's desires to the limits of what he is able to or wants to contain in the therapeutic action of psychoanalysis.

I believe that the patient's experience of the analyst's acknowledged and unacknowledged limits in bearing experience is undertheorized in psychoanalysis. I also believe that the ways these limits are repeated in the transference-countertransference is also undertheorized. In this chapter, I try to illustrate how the experience of limit is part of a dense undercurrent within the object relation between patient and analyst, a density that sometimes gives rise to shifts in the capacity to bear affects linked to the unsatisfying internal object relation. This chapter is part of a broader trend among contemporary authors to revisit some of Klein's and Winnicott's revolutionary insights in light of a greater appreciation of the analyst's contribution to the analytic process (e.g. Civitarese, 2008; Cooper, 2000, 2018, 2019; Fabozzi, 2016; Feldman, 1998; Ogden, 1982, 2010, 2016; Roussillon, 2011; Wilson, 2013).

Most important to my argument is that the patient's and the analyst's experiences of limit are hopefully "in play" during the process of the patient's working through his or her relation to the bad object. This relation to the patient's internal objects is where play itself begins. "Play" stands in contrast to "release," since play is contingent on the enduring internalized bad object as play partner with the patient and analyst. This involves the patient's relation to his or her own internal world, the analyst's relation to his or her own internal world, and the intersubjective experience of trying to know the patient's inner world together. The analyst's attempt to make use of his own thoughts about limit will often influence a patient's capacity to take in a new part of his or her experience. More generally, I try to pay attention to the patient's awareness of the analyst's relationship to the patient's *internal objects*, including love, frustration, patience, impatience, anger, envy, and admiration. The analyst's established capacity for containment is a necessary prerequisite for the patient to make use of the analyst's limit in the play between patient and analyst.

While a great deal of psychoanalysis has focused on Winnicott's (1951) formulation of the holding elements of transitional space and play, I emphasize that the concept of limit is also constitutive of play. As depicted in his emphasis on the analyst's hate in the countertransference, for Winnicott the concept of limit was essential to understanding influential elements of the analytic setting in facilitating play (Winnicott, 1949). For example, Winnicott's (1945) understanding that the analyst of a depressed patient must cope with his own "guilt and grief resultant from the destructive elements of his own (the analyst's) love" (p. 147) implicitly recognized the concept of limit. The analyst must always work with the limits of his own relation to internal objects in order to understand the things the patient carries (Cooper, 2014).

Here is an extended vignette through which I hope to illustrate how these limits bring us into a less desexualized (Green, 1975) version of Winnicott's theory of play, one in which collisions between two minds and the limits of two minds are in play. The patient's and analyst's awareness of these limitations and the attempt to make use of this awareness can help the patient accept an enlarging reality outside their internalized reality of unsatisfying or bad objects.

Henry: Part I

The material in this section summarizes Henry's first three years of analysis, highlighting some of the important rigid transference-countertransference configurations that opened to different kinds of exploration in the final two years of work.

Henry was a 25-year-old, single graduate student when I began working with him. We worked together in analysis four times a week for five years before he moved to another city to take on a tenure-track professorship there. A handsome man, Henry was slightly irritable around the edges, but he had a warmth and mildly melancholic way about him. He sought treatment because he was quite angry with his father and wanted to try to work through some of the disappointment that he had felt with him. He also felt irritable toward his mother and guilty about his irritability with her limitations.

Henry was the older of two boys, three years apart. Henry had felt angry with his mother during his adolescence on several different scores. As a child, he had felt that his mother was warm and physically responsive to him. They would do fun outdoor activities together such as swim and ride horses. Henry had explicit memories of being extremely sexually excited to be in his mother's presence alone in his parents' bedroom. He would watch her undress, possibly rubbing himself, and in retrospect he wonders if his mother didn't understand how exciting this was for him as a very small boy. Henry would often feel dropped by his mother when his father would return from work. As I listened to Henry's pain about being dropped, I had the sense that this included but went well beyond an Oedipal rivalry with his father for his mother's attention. Henry sensed that his mother felt that she had to organize all of her actions around her husband's need to be the center of attention.

Henry's father was a successful attorney and managing partner at his law firm. Henry felt that his father engaged his mind in ways that his mother did not, especially through the science, and politics. However, his father seemed to always take up the oxygen in the room, demanding to be the center of attention in discussion. At other times, his father seemed sullen and Henry felt that his father was lost in a world of reading and music. Henry saw no port of entry and felt alone.

When I first listened to Henry describe his anger toward his father, I was struck that it was as though his parents were a unit, each stimulating his anger and disappointment. His father's need to be the focus made him angry, but he was furious about his mother's passivity and her recruitment of Henry to help her feel secure and safe. I suggested that he might be angry at her partly because she exemplified some feelings of passivity and submission within himself that he was ashamed of and dreaded.

An important part of Henry's analysis involved a memory of his transitional object, a teddy bear from early life who became part of the play that emerged as he was about six years old. Henry recalled that he would frequently imagine scenarios with his teddy bear in which he, Henry, was a very good cowboy who always tried to do the right thing. In the play that emerged when he was alone, Henry was approached by an authority figure like a town sheriff or mayor (the bear) who accused Henry of doing something that he hadn't done. Everyone else around him, such as the people in the town, believed the sheriff, and Henry was very hurt and very, very angry. At some point he yelled at the sheriff and said, "You're lying. You're bad and I'm good. I'm telling the truth and you're not." The teddy bear/ sheriff, who was angry about what Henry was accusing him of, attacked Henry and knocked him to the ground. Henry got up on his feet and whaled into the sheriff. They went back and forth hitting each other, knocking each other down, until finally, Henry prevailed and said to the sheriff, "Tell them the truth. Have you been lying? Aren't you the bad one? Aren't I the good one?" And finally, the sheriff in his exhaustion and fear admitted to everyone that he was doing many bad things and blaming Henry. Henry was victorious and vindicated.

Henry felt that he was especially prone to enact this form of play when he was alone in his room after getting in trouble with his father for misbehaving or being falsely accused of it by his brother. Throughout his analysis we returned to this scenario. I understood with him that he and his mother might have been like the unsuspecting townspeople in his teddy bear turned sheriff play—a form of play in which the townspeople falsely believed that the sheriff was good, blamed Henry, and failed to do something about it until Henry's triumphant reveal.

When Henry began seeing me, he told me that he had met with a few analysts in order to decide with whom he wanted to work. He liked that he felt a close, almost "tribal connection" to me because we had similar builds and appearance. He also said provocatively that he liked that I had published and "that maybe you're enough of an asshole like my father that I can get into it with you." From the get-go, it seemed that Henry formed an alliance with me that included banter about the link between his father's ambition and narcissism and mine. Whether this was about my "real" narcissism or his fantasy of how it played out inside me was ambiguous.

Seen from the perspective of play and its central importance in psychoanalysis, Henry found a man, also a play object, with whom he could be angry and call out his father's narcissism. I could feel how much I was being asked to absorb his anger toward his parents, his father in particular, and that his attitude toward me contrasted with how buttoned up he actually was with his father. The structure of his obedience and deference to his father was still quite intact during much of our work.

Particularly during the first several years of our work, I could sometimes feel a deep mutual affection in addition to his sarcastic distrust. It seemed that he was hedging his bet through his humor, and it was only I who could hold that there was something good and affectionate between us. His clear commitment to his analysis was always punctuated by self-effacing remarks about how pathetic he was for feeling attached to his analysis and to me. This self-reproach and shame alternated with many negative comments about what he termed sycophantic younger colleagues coming and going from my office. When he was most depressed and angry, I could feel the sting. Again, I suggested that he feared that he would be submitting to me were he to allow for something positive between us. He envied the good feelings that he imagined went on between these other patients and me.

He would also paint mocking pictures of a few of his male professors in his graduate department that were quite cutting, and served as partial depictions of the transference. Usually the themes were about how they were aging, "nerdy," successful but narcissistically vulnerable men preoccupied with being sexually appealing. I tried to articulate how much letting in good, trusting feelings between us catalyzed his fear that, like the unsuspecting townspeople in his childhood play, he was acting like his mother or himself in acclimating to his father. He would be getting suckered into something. It "sucked" to be him in this dependent position, passive and setting himself up to be hurt. Most of his relationships with women to whom he was strongly attracted also involved this dynamic in which he felt it was a matter of time before he discovered that they were toying with him.

In a particular hour from late in his third year of analysis, Henry began by describing one of his fantasies in which he imagined the professor at home having a masturbation fantasy about having sex with two female students. During sex the female students are reciting observations from their field of study until they and the professor reach orgasm. In Henry's fantasy, the two female students were going along with the whole thing because they felt that they had to appease the professor lest he hurt their careers. It seemed to me that he was constructing an internalized picture of his feminized position in relation to his father's libidinization of power within the family. The fantasy captured submission and private revenge for himself and for his mother.

I suggested to Henry that he felt that his father had made all the rules, leaving him powerless, and that in the same way, he felt unable to make any of the rules with me. I also commented that in a less straightforward way, he partly empowered his female colleagues— and therefore, perhaps, himself and his mother—to use the professor and not only be abused by the professor's/father's malignant narcissism. I wondered with him whether in this fantasy he was making some of his own rules and not just allowing the father figures to make the rules. I also commented on the obvious way that there was a part of himself that felt a link to these women and to his mother in relationship to his father. He said, "You mean I feel feminized. Yup."

Henry then did what he often did during the first three years of our work when he thought that I said something meaningful to him—he quickly turned it into a point of sarcasm. He said, "You always surprise me when you tell me something that I didn't already think of." Then he became quiet for a moment and seemed sad. After the silence Henry then associated to how often his father would rail at the dinner table about a grievance against their condo and his partners at work. Henry said that he felt liked a trapped prisoner at the dinner table listening to these rants and that his mother would often look dissociated.

As the hour ended, Henry associated to some fantasies that he had spoken of recently in which a figure suddenly arrives at his house to do an intervention or remove his father and put him under what he called "psychological arrest." Henry pointedly said, knowing that the opposite was true, "And this person was NOT you." This fantasy aligned with some earlier and current dreams that I will turn to shortly.

In this hour, Henry was clearly feeling a greater capacity for play with his rage and sadness toward his father. His fantasies expressed a wish to create some of his own rules regarding feeling less tyrannized by his father. There is also a simultaneous experience of anger toward me in the transference for my rules in the analytic setting as well as gratitude (in the silence) for the way he experiences me trying help him work through his rage toward his father.

Shortly after the session that I have summarized, Henry returned to two dreams from childhood that he had relayed earlier in the analysis. The first was a very pleasurable dream of floating on a cloud made of pancakes with his father. He felt safe, warm, and cozy with his father. Was this an Oedipal form of detente in which he and his father can both float on his mother's pancake breast? I also wondered whether his associations to these dreams now suggested more of his disavowed love and tenderness for me. As mentioned earlier, interpretations of emergent good feelings toward me engendered shame and/or denial so I held for now from making that link.

The other dream occurred when he was about eight years old. In the dream, an old family friend, a close friend of his father, Gerhard, had come and handed him the remains of his father. He handed Henry two seeds, which he said were his father's eyes. Henry was horrified but it was clear that his family friend had done something that Henry wanted done. He had killed the bad man in Henry's mind. Henry was very sad to lose his father and ashamed of the relief he felt about the murder. Gerhard was a man of mischief who sometimes played fun, pretend chase games with Henry and his brother.

Gerhard took a very strong interest in Henry on shared family vacations. Gerhard had an intuitive way of jousting with and challenging Henry's father. After associating to this dream, Henry begrudgingly linked Gerhard to me as someone who could more playfully find Henry and help him with his anger toward his father. I was buoyed by Henry's ability to be less ashamed about giving voice to these tender feelings. We'd been playing lots of chase in this analysis.

As analysis deepened, and his unacknowledged trust in me seemed to grow, often Henry's dreams involved themes of Henry being dominated. Henry was staging in his dreams a deep anxiety about a precariousness that he had always felt about his father's approval and his anger toward his father about being required to submit. At the same time, it seemed that the more that we explored this deep anxiety about his fraught attachment to his father, the less Henry would devalue his mother. He was getting a better sense of who she was and how much his anger toward her involved a projection of some of his own anxiety about his attachment to his father. He hated in himself what he saw in his mother's anxiety.

This led to a more direct expression of fantasies in which Henry was prisoner and I was a sadistic prison warden or guard. Sometimes as the warden I was indifferent. Henry was a man without a name, only a number. I interpreted these fantasies as a form of closeness with his father, one that went hand in hand with tyranny, or as I put it to him, hand in chain. Sometimes Henry could verbally, explicitly link these feelings toward me with his experience of his father, and it was clear that internally he did so.

I disliked being seen in this way since my experience of Henry was one of tremendous fondness, but I knew that he was elaborating important parts of his attachment to his father. I was beginning to feel that there was something libidinally gratifying about trashing his father and me, holding on as it were to such a frustrating object. I felt a glimmer of fear that he would get stuck in his anger. I had felt that I had spent too long in unresolved angry and competitive feelings toward my own father as well as toward institutions that represented parental hypocrisy. Though I felt that Henry was working hard and growing, my fantasies of him becoming stuck in his anger were developing in concert with his growth.

Henry: Part 2

In the last two years of Henry's analysis there was an intensification of Henry's anger with his father, devaluation of me, and the intermittent emergence of tenderness toward me and positive transference. In line with Wilson's (2013) observation that countertransference is an activity, I will elaborate some clinical material focused on my countertransference and its relation to some of the working through of Henry's anger.

Henry started to have a more serious relationship with a woman. She didn't fit into his usual experiences of intriguing and unavailable or boring and available. She was interesting, attractive and available to know him and be known. Three or four months after beginning his relationship with her, Henry described a series of sexual fantasies in some detail that were sometimes realized in their relationship. He felt that the fantasies were fun, compelling, and organized by mutual play and gratification. Along the way there was lots of domination and submission.

In the fantasy, Henry and his girlfriend would take turns penetrating each other during intercourse. The fantasy begins with Henry penetrating his girlfriend through intercourse. At some point, he asks her if he can penetrate her anally and she smiles and says "No, maybe later." Then she turns him over on his stomach and climbs on top of him with a strap-on. She penetrates him and they are both extremely excited until Henry comes. There were a number of variations of this fantasy and, as I said, some of these were realized in their actual sexual life. In reality though, while his girlfriend was open to penetrating him, she was not very excited by it and Henry less excited in the realization than in the fantasy. Henry so appreciated her willingness to try it; even more, he appreciated that he was beginning to feel like he could say so much more to her about his feelings, desires, and fantasies.

This was an interesting turn because for the first time, less controlled by shame, Henry was able to link how much he appreciated being able to say whatever came to mind with his girlfriend with how he felt in analysis. It felt like a quantum leap to tolerate a tenderness with which he had not been on speaking terms, either within himself or in dialogue with me.

Henry and I spent many sessions trying to understand some of his sexual fantasies. I suggested to him that I thought that the fantasies were gratifying on a few scores. First, he wanted to feel that his mother was assertive and empowered enough to penetrate his mind. Henry's younger brother irrepressibly insisted that his mother know him and listen to his thoughts. In contrast, Henry wanted to feel his mother's desire to know him and felt aggrieved by passivity about knowing him. I was also struck that the structure of his desire and romantic longings had moved from conviction that in a romantic relationship someone is getting fucked or fucked over toward a trust that emotional and sexual penetration could be enjoyed.

Henry's dreams began to change, now involving male mentors who were more explicitly helping him with his work and scholarship. I took up the dreams as related to a feeling of being helped in the analysis, but Henry could only tolerate brief moments of tenderness and gratitude toward me before returning to his anger at his father and intermittent mockery of me. I experienced his anger as an atavistic, unnecessary psychic appendage from earlier psychic development despite knowing that it was there partly as a way to hold on to his attachment to his father. I found myself increasingly feeling a kind of non-relatedness and mild dissociation in response to Henry's anger. It is this aspect of my countertransference that will now be my focus.

I decided to consult with a close female colleague about my then recent sense of remove regarding Henry's persisting anger toward his father. We discussed some of my conscious concerns that Henry might become stuck in his grievance, unconsciously staying in his fraught attachment to the father and self he knew. I also told her that sometimes I thought that he was building a world in which he could institute the analysis as a holding place for his father to be prosecuted in court. She wondered whether I might consider telling him that there was something about his relentless anger toward his father that was making me feel less curious or interested. I felt that I didn't want to say this to Henry, but her remarks resonated for me as something to understand better, particularly because I was immediately uncomfortable.

I had two associations during the consultation with my colleague, both seemingly related to a fantasy of my patient's permanent prosecution of a case against his father. One was to an Argentinian film, The Secret in their Eyes (2009), in which a man whose wife has been killed finds her killer, who has escaped justice. The husband secretly imprisons him in his house, seeking justice since the corrupt authorities had not acted.

The other association was to an old joke about envy. A Russian farmer is constantly coveting his neighbor's cow. A Russian genie of sorts comes along and says to the farmer," I'll grant you anything you want. Would you like me to grant you a new cow of your own just like your neighbor's?" And the farmer, after initially declining, replies, "Well on second thought my wish is not that you would get me a cow of my own, but would you please kill my neighbor's cow?" This is the essence of grievance as resistance to grieving—the unconscious or conscious attempt to institutionalize grievance rather than mourning loss and disappointment. The farmer deprives himself in order to continue prosecuting a case.

I felt strongly that I needed to consider my resistance to what my colleague suggested. Why was I unable to play with the limits of my attention and interest in Henry's persistent anger in a way that might yield something new? On the face of it, I was concerned that I would be minimizing Henry's opportunity to work through his angry feelings toward his father and the negative part of the transference with me. But I was also clearly dissociated and my reverie in response to the consultation involved many themes of domination, control, and sadistic revenge. If the consultant was outlining a limit for me in terms of trying too hard to abide Henry's persistent anger, perhaps I was resisting this limit myself. I was sometimes aware of a part of me that identified with Henry's anger and competitive feelings toward parental authority. Was I resisting what she was seeing in a way that paralleled Henry's resistance to what I was seeing and feeling in him?

I also recall having a set of associations in the week or two following my colleague's help related to how she was penetrating my mind and feelings. Had I found a good mother or parent with an active mind—not a dissociated mind, which was the part of Henry's mother that was so saddening and enraging for him? I thought so and yet I also resisted the impulse to implement her suggestion for fear of insufficiently containing Henry's anger. For a few more months of analysis, there were intermittent periods of railing against his father and I continued to feel a sense of non-relatedness. One day these words came to my mind for seemingly an instant before I found that I had said them: "How much more of this anger will you court?" I say, "seemingly an instant" because I was aware that I held myself back from saying "indulge" and instead used an uncommon word for me, "court." I did not want to criticize him, but I think I did in some way formalize the message through the word "court," creating distance even as I was trying to do something quite different and, in a sense, quite intimate.

Henry was stunned for an instant and then started laughing, at first uncomfortably and then genuinely laughing. Henry said: "Well, somebody is feeling peppy this morning."

After a pause, he said defiantly, "The answer to your question is no, I haven't had enough." I was quiet and Henry grew unusually quiet. Naturally I was concerned that I had shut him down. He then said, "I don't think that I've ever felt as close to you as I do right now."

Me:	Can you say more?
Henry:	"I could actually feel you being with me as a person. I felt that you were talking to me like I imagine you speaking with your wife or your children. Maybe you're telling me that you've had enough of my complaining about my father."
Me:	"I sometimes feel worried about whether you will be able to feel less angry, but I don't actually want you to stop talking about everything that you feel. I've recently noticed in myself a kind of distancing and glazing over when you're speaking about your dad. I always understand your well-justified anger toward him. I think that I've been worried that you might stay stuck in this position of grievance toward him without mourning how he has affected you."
Henry:	"What makes you say I'm not mourning?"
Me:	(feeling myself in agreement with Henry and a bit embarrassed by his correcting me): "Maybe you are mourning. You're right. But you're mourning while still trying to keep your anger alive. As bad as he was, it seems like you need him to be that bad guy. He's the only guy you had. And you still think that you must be a bad guy and you aren't.

	And sometimes I feel like you need me to be a bad guy, your bad guy."
Henry:	"Fair enough. I want to punish him. I guess it's at my own expense. I know it is. (Pause) I've never thought this before but when I'm angry like this it actually reminds me of my father."
Henry continues:	"You know when you said that to me, I didn't feel like your prisoner. I didn't feel like this analysis was a weird, isolated prison cell. I felt like you spoke to me as my father—well, not my father but a different kind of father, as my friend. I liked it." He then said something dismissive about my not getting any fancy ideas.

And so went our analysis, back and forth with grievance and moments in which Henry seemed to be allowing that he could be a good man and that I could be a good man with him. I was able to better listen to his anger again, too, which of course did not entirely vanish. Over the final year of his analysis, I came to appreciate that Henry's silences reflected his love of me and his potential shame about submission to his father. I began much more directly asking why he'd grown silent when he insulted me, venturing that he felt guilty about needing to attack me when he felt grateful. A turning point in Henry's treatment occurred when he expressed more directly the vulnerability he would feel if he were to stop "giving me shit," and that he didn't really want to act that way anymore. I told him that I thought that he loved his father intensely, and that he loved me too, and that he needed to hold on to the ways that I was linked to the parts of his father that he loved and hated. If he just took in the good parts, something good that I had said or been able to understand, he would be losing the bad parts, which he was also attached to, even if he hated them. He wanted to "give me the shit" he held on to and he also didn't.

Even later still, a few times when Henry started in on insulting me in what seemed like gratuitous ways, I simply said to him, "Were you to stop that, I wonder what else you might feel that you hold at bay?" Echoing his earlier observation when I had asked him about "how much more of this anger will you court," he said, "I didn't think that analysts were supposed to tell their patients not to say what comes to mind." I said, "That's mostly true, but I think that you can actually bear your angry and hurt feelings toward your father that you feel with me along with your loving and warm feelings toward us both. You can hate me all you want but it doesn't mean that I always feel like putting up with it." Again, he laughed, and he spoke of how much time he felt that he might be wasting. I thought to myself about how much work had gone into being able to speak to each other in this way. I also had the thought that perhaps Henry had found a safe place to hate which allowed him a safer place to love.

Discussion

I have examined an area of participation that has been less of a focus in our literature. One of our most important ways of conveying our limits to patients and ourselves is through the structure of the analytic setting itself. Paradoxically, the rules of the analytic process generate one of the highest forms of intimacy in analysis. I have tried to elaborate a context in which the analyst's attempt to analyze his own understanding of limit influences a patient's capacity to take in new experience.

In my work with Henry I made use of my resistance to understanding more deeply his refractory grievance and attachment to a bad object. Sometimes the main volume of work for the analyst in this context is internal and involves the transformation of their own dissociative states into an understanding of the patient's dissociated states relative to their grievance. Yet the work is always occurring in an intersubjective context, one in which our resistance to working with limit as well as our process of working through that resistance to limit are conveyed to patients.

I think it is most useful to frame my dissociation as a resistance to finding play with my own limits in working with Henry's fraught and ambivalent relationship to his internal objects. There were several forms of resistance to playing with my own limits. I was to some degree unconsciously identified with Henry's anger toward his father. I was also quite worried that conveying my limits either through interpretation or directly might be destructive. This "concern," though, may have acted as a double agent, serving to preserve my hidden conspiratorial alliance with Henry's outrage and his attachment to the bad object. The consultant was trying to help me make use of my own limits in ways that honor how limit is constitutive of play. I was resisting her technical suggestion, a suggestion that was a kind of broad template that had many potentially creative ways of being implemented.

Put another way, my resistance to the consultant ran parallel to Henry's contempt, his impulses to frustrate, his fears of being dominated and feeling vulnerable, and his defenses against receiving something good. I had lost a position of understanding that considers how, as Harris (2017, p. 895) put it, "Intimacy is the contradictory site of freedom and regulation." We could posit that my consultant was not just a good maternal object or subject with whom I could be a good object/analyst or subject. As I have suggested in an earlier paper (Cooper, 2004), she was also a "bad" object/subject with whom I could be a bad object/subject (he who felt limits). This kind of "bad" object is a new object and extremely helpful. Play occurs when seemingly opposing elements can operate synergistically (Benjamin, 2004), rather than antagonistically, creating new possibilities for intimacy and self-assertion. Splits between good and bad can yield to a new appreciation of how we need all of our objects, and none of them are going away.

I believe that Henry's early childhood play with his teddy bear as sheriff and his play with me as his prisoner were enacted in certain ways in the point of repetition or impasse that I am describing. The notion of the good sheriff underscores how much Henry had not been able to use his father as a benign limiting force in the development of his superego. His continued tendency to rail against his father suggests identification with the angry part of his father rather than with a more benign regulation of his inner life. The themes of sadism, punishment and revenge were enacted in Henry's holding on to his anger. He was both imprisoned by it and imprisoned by me, demanding like this father that he be bound to us. In retrospect, I believe that my expressing the limits of my attention to Henry was an entry into Henry's childhood room, interrupting his tirade at Teddy/sheriff/daddy and putting my arms around him as if to say: "That's enough. Let's do something different." I became part of a more benevolent superego after having been the bad, enraging father.

Henry's gradual associative freedom in the analysis and his growing trust allowed him to see his mother in new ways. Eventually his new loving relationship with a woman permitted new forms of transforming sadism and revenge into sexual play and new sexual drive-state experiences of himself. He was freer to associate and allow new forms of play with his enduring anger. These new drive-states and capacities for sexual fantasy and play in Henry also allowed me greater understanding of my fears of my own aggression toward Henry in expressing limit. This led me to move away from dissociation and toward my colleague's suggested direction. Rather than exorcise the bad object, I think that Henry and I were each able to make use of our bad objects and stop needing in paralyzing, inflexible ways to split them off from our good objects.

The concept of limit is interesting to think about with regard to maternal and paternal limits. Winnicott (1945, 1969) addressed the limits of maternal preoccupation but his focus on intersubjective engagement mostly centered on the mother's acclimation to the infant's subjectivity. Benjamin (1988) interrogated the implications of maternal subjectivity (love and hate) and, by implication, maternal limits, in a way that expanded Winnicott's intersubjective field between infant and child. Chatrite-Vatine (2014) has elaborated a limit-setting function of the mother, involving both the seductive and ethical elements of the psychoanalytic situation.

Freud (1923, 1924) focused primarily on paternal limits associated with superego development in the context of Oedipal development. Herzog (2001) emphasized "father hunger" (Herzog, 2001), a set of needs that involve a more primary need for a father. I suggest that I was holding and containing Henry's rage while operating as a kind of benign, auxiliary superego in a way that his father could not since he was such a simultaneously weak and frightening object for Henry. Yet I was also limited in my own capacities to serve this benign function since it was mitigated by my identification with Henry as an aggrieved son. From the perspective of Corbett's (under review) recent examination of paternal eroticism, Henry's work with me allowed us to discover a more supple and creative re-signification of paternity in contrast to a rigidified and split (good versus bad) experience of his father.

To some extent, I am trying to further explore some of the terrain that Symington (1983) elaborated in his work on the analyst's personal "act of freedom." Symington examined how some modes of interpretation emanate from the transition from being a fused object in the transference to a separate one. The interpretation is essential in that it gives expression to the shift that has already occurred and makes it available to consciousness. There are many clinical examples in the literature which implicitly bring the analyst's limits into play (e.g. Parsons, 1999, 2007). Our theory of this component of play has lagged behind our clinical use of limit in the therapeutic action of psychoanalysis. Ogden (1994) also implicitly explores the area of limit in his work on "interpretive action" in which he addresses places where interpretation itself has been incorporated into elements of the patient's unconscious mind. In such instances he documents the use of particular kinds of action in order to create an outside space for the patient's reflection that interpretation alone is no longer able to provide.

The analyst's limitations in being attentive to the patient's affective experience sometimes reflect the patient's durable and frustrating attempt to institutionalize their suffering and attachment to their internal objects even as they are trying to metabolize these experiences. We might even speculate that the analyst is experiencing a kind of signal anxiety regarding the dangers of grievance being institutionalized as an adaptive affliction rather than worked through. Fortunately, we are also brought into some of the patient's capacities for play and for being helped by others. At times, our becoming more explicit about our own thinking regarding limit facilitates the patient's efforts to understand the demands of the setting. These demands are constructed to help the patient bear the loss accompanying the notion that analysis partly resides outside their internal life. These limits also ensure that the analyst will try to provide containment and understanding for their patients.

Much work/play occurs at the limits of what patient and analyst can express and tolerate. For example, Henry used humor as a kind of Trojan horse for transit to express and titrate his developing affection for and dependency on me. He had to laugh or mildly devalue my attempts to know him, particularly those that hit their mark. Analysts often learn how to find the moving target of patient's efforts to express and titrate what is being defended against. Schafer (1968) referred to this double edge of defenses as "double agents."

I speculate that the sexual abstinence required of both patient and analyst in the analytic process has occupied more conspicuously our theorization of the analyst's limits in the analytic process. Our abstinence is a shiny object for patient and analyst as a signifier of limit. Ironically, however, the transition of psychoanalysis to a focus on attachment and early object relations, and what Green (2008) described as the de-sexualization of analysis that he attributes to Fairbairn and Winnicott (unfairly I believe), belies a much larger problem regarding the analyst's limits. Perhaps we have had a harder time discussing the analyst's limits concerning matters other than sexual abstinence or offshoots of sexual abstinence. In some sense, we need to more fully illuminate limits on our psychoanalytic utopianism. Maybe we have even had an embedded fantasy of not having limits as analysts or not discussing them enough in the open. As Green (1975, p. 9) put it so succinctly,

> We can say that the analytic situation is the totality of the elements making up the analytic relationship, at the heart of which we can, in the course of time, observe a process whose knots are tied by the transference and the countertransference, due to the establishment and the limits of the analytic setting.

It is not Winnicott's fault, as our most important setting theorist, that psychoanalysts have too often equated psychoanalytic play with vaguely defined elements of transitional space. The robustness of the play concept resides in the way that play is set up, reconstructed, and always being renegotiated through the reality of limits. These limits as constitutive of play bring us deeply into questions of sexuality and drive states. It is also true that as early as 1945, Winnicott was elaborating an embedded theory that without working through his own relationship to his internal objects, the analyst is unable to help the patient with his or her internal objects. Implicitly then, Winnicott (1945) was understanding that only when the analyst can experience the limits of his own love and hate (Winnicott, 1949) can he or she know another, the patient. In this way, the setting and the objects in the setting, including the sense of limit, are always in dynamic relationship to one another (Cooper, 2019). For that matter, the implications of my argument here are that the concepts of limit and potential space are themselves in dynamic relation to one another rather than opposites.

Among the important reasons that new objects in psychoanalysis hold value is that they fuel our capacities to integrate play and excitement with the frustration intrinsic to all object relations. The intimacy of limit and the limit of intimacy activate each other as they are deeply partnered in the setting of psychoanalysis.

References

Benjamin, J. (1988) *The Bonds of Love: Psychoanalysis, Feminism, and the Problem of Domination*. New York: Pantheon Books.

Benjamin, J. (2004) Beyond doer and done to: An intersubjective view of thirdness. *Psychoanal. Q.* 73: 5–46.

Chatrite-Vatine, V. (2014) *The Ethical Seduction of the Analytic Situation: The Feminine-Maternal Origins of Responsibility for the Other*. London: Karnac Books, Ltd.

Civitarese, G. (2008) *The Intimate Room: Theory and Technique of the Analytic Field*. London: Routledge.

Cooper, S. H. (2000) *Objects of Hope: Exploring Possibility and Limit in Psychoanalysis*. Hillsdale, NJ: The Analytic Press.

Cooper, S. H. (2004) State of the hope: The new bad object in psychoanalysis. *Psychoanal. Dial.* 14: 527–551.

Cooper, S. H. (2014) The things we carry: Finding/creating the object and the analyst's self-reflective participation. *Psychoanal. Dial.* 24(6): 621–636.

Cooper, S. H. (2015) Reflections on the analyst's 'good enough' capacity to bear disappointment with special attention to repetition. *J. Amer. Psychoanal. Assn.* 63: 1193–1213.

Cooper, S. H. (2018) Playing in the darkness: Use of the object and use of the subject. *J. Amer. Psychoanal. Assn.* 66(4): 743–765.

Cooper, S. H. (2019) A theory of the setting: The transformation of unrepresented experience and play. *Int. J. Psycho-Anal.* 100: 1439–1454.

Cooper, S. H. and Levit, D. B. (1998) Old and new objects in Fairbairnian and American relational theory. *Psychoanal. Dial.* 8(5): 603–624.

Corbett, K. (Unpublished manuscript, under review) The paternal erotic transference-countertransference.

Fabozzi, P. (2016) The use of the analyst and the sense of being real: The clinical meaning of Winnicott's "The Use of an Object". *Psychoanal Q.* 85(1): 1–34.

Fairbairn, W. R. D. (1943) The repression and return of bad objects (with special reference to the 'war neuroses'. In: *Psychoanalytic Studies of the Personality* (pp. 59–81). London: Routledge and Kegan Paul.

Fairbairn, W. R. D. (1958) On the nature and aims of psychoanalytical treatment. *Int. J. Psycho-Anal.* 39: 374–385.

Feldman, M. (1998) Projective identification: The analyst's contribution. *Int. J. Psychoanal.* 78: 227–241.

Freud, S. (1923) The ego and the id. *S.E.* 19.1–100.

Freud, S. (1924) The dissolution of the Oedipus complex. *S.E.* 19.173–179.

Green, A. (1975) The analyst, symbolization, and absence in the analytic setting – in memory of D. W. Winnicott. *Int. J. Psycho-Anal.* 56: 9–22.

Green, A. (2008) *The Chains of Eros: The Sexual in Psychoanalysis*. London: Routledge.

Harris, A. (2017) Intimacy: The tank in the bedroom. *Int. J. Psycho-Anal.* 98: 895–907.

Herzog, J. (2001) *Father Hunger: Explorations with Adults and Children*. Hillsdale, NJ: The Analytic Press.

Nacht, S. (1963) The non-verbal relationship in psycho-analytic treatment. *Int. J. Psycho-Anal.* 44: 333–354.

Ogden, T. H. (1982) *Projective Identification and Psychotherapeutic Technique*. New York: Jason Aronson.

Ogden, T. H. (1994) The concept of interpretive action. *Psychoanal. Q.* 63: 219–245.

Ogden, T. H. (2010) Why read Fairbairn. *Int. J. Psycho-Anal.* 91: 101–118.

Ogden, T. H. (2016) Destruction reconceived: On Winnicott's 'The Use of an Object and Relating through Identifications'. *Int. J. Psycho-Anal.* 97(5): 1243–1262.

Ogden, T. H. (2019) Ontological psychoanalysis or "What do you want to be when you grow up? *Psychoanal. Q.* 88(4): 661–694.

Parsons, M. (1999) The logic of play in psychoanalysis. *Int. J. Psycho-Anal.* 80(5): 871–884.

Parsons, M. (2007) Raiding the inarticulate: The internal analytic setting and listening beyond countertransference. *Int. J. Psycho-Anal.* 88(6):1441–1456.

Roussillon, R. (2011) *Primitive Agony and Symbolization*. London: Routledge.

Schafer, R. (1968) The mechanisms of defense. *Int. J. Psycho. Anal.* 49: 49–62.

Steiner, J. (2006) Interpretive enactments and the analytic setting. *Int. J. Psycho-Anal.* 87: 315–328.

Symington, N. (1983) The analyst's act of freedom as agent of therapeutic change. *Int. R. Psycho-Anal.* 10: 283–291.

Wilson, M. (2006) "Nothing could be further from the truth": The role of lack in the analytic process. *J. Amer. Psychoanal. Assn.* 54(2): 397–429.

Wilson, M. (2013) Desire and responsibility: The ethics of counter-transference experience. *Psychoanal. Q.* 82: 435–476.

Winnicott, D. W. (1945) Primitive emotional development. In: *Through Paediatrics in Psychoanalysis* (pp. 145–156). New York: Basic Books.

Winnicott, D. W. (1949) Hate in the countertransference. In: *Through Paediatrics in Psychoanalysis* (pp. 194–203). New York: Basic Books.

Winnicott, D. W. (1969) The use of an object. *Int. J. Psycho-Anal.* 50: 711–716.

Chapter 4

The Paradox of Play
in Mourning

The play of psychoanalysis, always embedded in transference countertransference process, sometimes helps edge patients from stultifying attachment to internalized objects toward potential mourning.
Play facilitates movement from the chains binding the self to an internal object, toward new experience with self and other.

I will address how play helps us to transform our melancholic relationships with objects into the possibility for mourning. Freud (1917)
charted how in melancholia painful experiences of loss are truncated or
denied through identification with the object. Rather than experience
loss, the person with melancholia denies separateness of the object.
Loss is omnipotently replaced through the ego's identification with the
object and essentially through the creation of an internal object
(Fairbairn, 1952; Ogden, 2012). It is often the case that the patient does
not know that there is an object that is lost. The melancholic is also
often not aware of what it is that he has lost in himself as a consequence
of maintaining attachment to the object. Productive play in psychoanalysis paradoxically awakens the sense of loss of self or of aspects of
an undeveloped self that have been previously denied.

I qualify here that I am primarily focusing on the way that patients
hold on to internal objects, partly as a mode of psychic survival and
partly as a resistance to new experience. Various self-states develop in
association with holding on to these internal objects, states that are
sequestered and sometimes emerge in analytic work (e.g. Benjamin,
2016; Davies, 2004). The transference as a container of old and new
experience becomes a useful crucible for expanding play in relationship to old objects even as it introduces a new relationship to self and

DOI: 10.4324/9781003265078-5

other. Part of the problem for patients who hold on to early, frustrating, and depriving objects is that their attachment to these early objects partly mitigates a sense of aloneness (Fairbairn, 1952).

Many patients come into analysis consciously or unconsciously trying to find a different relationship both with their analyst and with their old, persecutory bad objects. While analysts seek to help people become more themselves through analysis, these patients are often quite unaware of self apart from their identifications with objects. Often their terror involves unformulated questions such as, "What self do I have without my attachment to this object?" or "What self do I have a right to have?" (e.g. Modell, 1975). The internal objects to be mourned are refractory to analysis because they have become institutionalized as the mediators of the patient's terror of abandonment. These internal objects also contribute to a diffuse identity.

Part of the work of analysis is to show the relentless manner in which the patient keeps unconsciously reviving the attachment to and identification with these objects. We hope that play shows up through transference-countertransference engagement to help the patient experience new ways to live and work with these attachments.

Introduction: Play and Mourning

Winnicott (1968) conceptualized psychoanalysis as "a highly sophisticated twentieth century phenomenon," performed by two people, patient and analyst, to facilitate finding play with old and new parts of self. Play is the "natural thing" (p. 41), and psychoanalysis is an invention that integrates play as part of therapeutic action.

Winnicott resisted the notion of a single meaning of the word "play" in his own writing and it has remained a more evocative rather than strictly defined concept. We might regard play as a kind of cluster concept in Wittgenstein's (1953) terms. It evokes multiple meanings in different social and clinical contexts. In Chapter 2, I offered a way of thinking of play in relation to transference-countertransference engagement. I suggested that play occurs at a moment of dawning awareness of transference-countertransference enactment within both patient and analyst. In particular, it may involve the patient's and analyst's new awareness of their own *resistance* to understanding transference-countertransference enactments of the patient's attachment to internal object relations.

With regard to the play of mourning, I also favor one of Winnicott's descriptions of playing that appears in his important paper on play, "Playing: Creative Activity and the Search for Self." He states: "It is in playing and only in playing that the individual child or adult is able to be creative and to use the whole personality, and it is only in being creative that the individual discovers the self" (Winnicott, 1968, p. 54). This creative possibility was also emphasized by Pizer (1996), Parsons (1999), and Ringstrom (2001) in highlighting how trust can be developed through what feel like more spontaneous responsiveness with sometimes quite traumatized patients.

Thus, I interpret Winnicott's notion of "discovering the self" as an ability for patient and analyst to freshly, or sometimes even for the first time, recognize and express various feelings in the transference-countertransference. The analyst may also develop a greater openness to understanding types of enactment of the patient's attachment to debilitating internal objects. Together, these new experiences form the basis for play, a transition toward the capacity for mourning, and the patient's ability to live more creatively.

While it is true that at one level of theoretical discourse, all transference is a form of play and all play is embedded in transference-countertransference enactment, the forms of play that I am describing involve unique moments of intersubjective engagement. Play permits the obscure rules of transference-countertransference fixity to be loosened, just as it marks how these obscure rules are now more visible to patient and analyst. I use the word "obscure" to get at the analyst's resistance to better understanding the dyad's rules of engagement and enactment in the transference-countertransference. In this kind of engagement, the patient and analyst are able to hear or experience a psychic or intersubjective reality in a new key. I will try to demonstrate some of these sorts of clinical moments in two vignettes and in a poem by Elizabeth Bishop about loss.

The matter of distinguishing transference and play is a thorny one since they are highly overlapping areas. After all, Freud (1914) used the term *tummelplatz* to describe transference, a term that translates to a "play area," "playground," "hotbed," or "battleground." Thus Freud's (1914) particular descriptions of transference sowed the seeds of appreciating the importance of play in psychoanalysis even before Winnicott elevated play to the basis of therapeutic action. Freud's reference to the transference as playground demarcates transference as the area between fantasy and reality. Transference borrows from the real and not real elements of an arrangement that patient and analyst surrender to and hopefully learn from. In transference, we play with the real person of the analyst but also one in effigy since the transference symbolizes other, earlier object relations. The illusions that are provided by transference catalyze wishes and desires revived on a daily basis in analytic work.

Winnicott's use of the term "play" borrows in various ways from Freud's conceptualization of transference. Winnicott's view of play also occurs between reality and fantasy. In my view, among the most important of Winnicott's discoveries was that play essentially picked up where Freud left off in "Remembering, Repeating and Working Through." In that paper Freud asserted that the transference is enacted before it can be expressed. Freud was describing how unconscious content that cannot yet be verbally articulated is enacted before it can be expressed. Freud's use of the term enactment (for the first time in the history of psychoanalysis) did not have a dyadic meaning but instead referred to how the transference is in action before it can be verbalized.

Winnicott's introduction of play provides a dyadic view of how, as transference is enacted, it may become accessible through the inter-subjective experience of patient and analyst in play. I view play as a kind of window into the obscure rules of transference-countertransference engagement, an opening at the seam between obscure rules and rules which have become illuminated. Green's (1975) term "ventilated spaces" applies to these moments of new awareness, a kind of transit from unrepresented states to greater representation.

It may seem counterintuitive to link play with mourning. Yet we know that play is not always associated with fun or a good time. For children and adults, forms of play are quite serious. Some forms of play involve the mastery of separation or loss (e.g. fort-da). Vygotsky (1934) explored the rule-bound foundations of play, positing that the external language that children hear and imitate is internalized during imaginative play. In a sense, play is being used by the child in development to help integrate reality. Free association itself may be viewed as a form of imaginative play, a new way of having internal and external dialogue and often with very new content. In the moments of play that I describe, we are able to budge our internalized rules and assist in mourning the loss of our old, psychically created rules. These rules were created in the context of early adaptation to the limitations of objects around us. Our psychically made up rules involve unconscious fantasies and the internalized object relations that accompany these fantasies. In Chapter 3, I argued that we have undertheorized the ways in which limit is constitutive of play and underemphasized the importance of limit in our readings of how Winnicott described play, illusion and potential space.

One form of play related to the capacity for mourning involves finding old parts of self, feelings, and "bits and pieces" (Winnicott, 1968) and seeing how they can be in conversation with new states of being. The mourning process often relates to elements of fantasy, identity, internal objects, and actual lost objects. Mourning is aided by the holding and containment of the analyst just as it catalyzes the experiences in the transference that often need to be mourned. Parallel to these activities in mourning is the way that play in forms of music and poetry become an essential part of funeral and death ceremonies. In the paradoxical density of play, functions of remembering and mitigating loss are active during these ceremonies.

Transference exists in past time and real time. In real time, psychoanalysis often aims to help the patient to experience the cost of not seeing the lost object or separating from the lost object. Sometimes grieving involves mourning the loss of an object relation that never was what the patient has internally created. Psychoanalysis also tries to make the experience of lost time something real before too much time has gone by and pathological mourning has set in through hypertrophied regret or nostalgia. In the clinical vignettes that I will present, play provides a transition from unconsciously held fantasies of loss (often elements of denial) to a better ability to integrate the actual loss of time or the cost of a constricted psychic life.

Psychoanalysis has long offered observations that indirectly refer to the relationship between play and mourning. Freud (1914, p. 14) described fort-da as an effort to master anxiety related to loss through play. Winnicott (1951) observed that the transitional object serves as a "not me" possession to both help embrace discovery and acceptance of the object world while simultaneously lessening separation anxiety. The loss of parental objects catalyzes the use of a transitional object, just as the transitional object facilitates the child's adaptation to loss. The child's sovereign rule of the "not me" possession restores an omnipotent fantasy of feeling connected to a caretaking other. Winnicott's observation of the transitional object put into focus that we cannot grow and experience newness without loss. By implication, play not only serves as a vehicle for working through loss but in some sense carries and signifies loss into newly found reality. Play is always helping us with mourning.

Winnicott (1951) shed further light on how play and mourning relate to one another. Winnicott states that the transitional object is neither repressed nor mourned but instead is diffused through our relationship to culture and religion. I view this statement as suggesting that mourning is not a discrete event. The transitional object and its residua are used through life to manage the loss of the early maternal environment and ensuing separation anxiety. If existence involves the perpetual task of separating internal and external reality as Winnicott (1951, 1969) suggests, we are also in an ongoing mourning of omnipotent fantasy.

In Winnicott's (1974) *Fear of Breakdown*, he weighs in on how the play of transference helps the patient to move past experiences, often those involving loss, into the present.

It must be asked here: why does the patient go on being worried by this that belongs to the past? The answer must be that the original experience of primitive agony cannot get into the past tense unless the ego can first gather it into its own present time experience and into omnipotent control now (assuming the auxiliary ego-supporting function of the mother [analyst]).

We could say that the play of the patient's transference in which failure is relived in vivo and enacted with the analyst is what brings the patient into present time. The analyst tries to find play in both repetition and through pointing out to the patient, "repeatedly," how the patient is carrying out this work of moving the past to the present in the analytic process (Cooper, 2015).

Parsons (1999) hinted at how play partly helps us to master traumatic situations by exploring them within a framework that makes them easier to bear. Play often involves a regressive element, which helps us to mourn earlier losses that are a part of any form of development.

Even though Loewald (1960) discusses therapeutic action in a manner that is not focused on play, he explicitly understands the dynamic tension between regression and development when he says that every good interpretation takes the patient one step into regression just as we anticipate a psychic future. While it is most often the patient who finds play in the service of mourning, the analyst's experience of the patient's futurity is itself a form of play and, in my view, one of the most important elements of the therapeutic action (Cooper, 1997; Griffin, 2020). It is as though the analyst is stating to the patient: "As you confront loss or de-identification with earlier objects, I can imagine a self that you have not yet fully experienced."

I will also explore the analyst's activity in the countertransference (e.g. Wilson, 2013) to find forms of play that facilitate the mourning process. Patient and analyst are inevitably enacting elements of this unchanged internalized attachment. Countertransference activity is often related to trying to understand how the patient and analyst shift in their relationship to internalized unsatisfying or punishing objects. Play occurs inside these enactments (e.g. Benjamin, 2016; Cooper, 2018) in which dissociated feelings are marked in new ways. In order to facilitate mourning, sometimes the analyst needs to gain better purchase on his own resistance to finding new forms of play in the patient's often repetitive and unsymbolized experiences. As Benjamin (2004, 2016) has noted, this is an essential part of a process of repair.

I now turn to an analysis of a poem by Elizabeth Bishop and two brief clinical examples to illustrate how play, often routine but subtly different, helps carry patient and analyst into the mourning process.

Elizabeth Bishop's "One Art": An Example of Play as a Link to Grieving

I will focus on some elements of play that simultaneously exemplify resistance to mourning and the capacity for mourning in the poem "One Art" (Bishop, 1994). Bishop suggests somewhat ironically that we might become masters of the art of losing and in so doing, find aspects of ourselves. The tone of the poem, however, suggests that the devastation of loss is always close behind and she knows that she has no chance. Play occurs in the shadow of loss and the trick is to be able to partially, gradually integrate loss without being devastated by it. Play occurs in Bishop's fantastic capacity to simultaneously hold both glibness and earnestness regarding loss. By the end of the poem, she has given herself over to the acknowledgment of loss of a loved one when she implores herself to write it that her loss, may look like a disaster.

In the poem, Bishop meditates on the art of losing, building up a small catalogue of losses, which include house keys and a mother's watch, before climaxing in the loss of houses, land, two continents, and a loved one. By calling the notion of losing as an art, she has used an omnipotent fantasy that she can control loss. She makes us wonder if she can perhaps even bring loss into being herself or if she is simply using it for her artistic purposes. In this form of fantasy, she has turned passive into active as a way to master loss and mitigate its accompanying pain. The play has occurred in trying on fantasies and experiences of loss as a master of loss, an artist practicing her craft. She is a fort-da child throwing away a reel of string and gathering it up as though losing homes, losing continents, and losing important others are really not such big losses.

Bishop considers losing as a form of practice. Instead of being the victim of loss, she thinks of it as a discipline of sorts that requires hard work and repeated experience. Obviously, there is sarcasm and glibness, but they are postured positions. Play resides more in the feigned wish to consider herself the creator or master of loss rather than subject to it.

The poem mirrors some elements of therapeutic action regarding grieving in that she is describing a way that, bit-by-bit, through small accretions we are able to integrate loss. In the last line of the poem, as she is finally able to more fully acknowledge that loss is not such a disaster, she continues to defensively mitigate loss by stating that loss might looks like a disaster rather it being a disaster. In Benjamin's (2016) terms, Bishop has been able to provide a metacommunication toward herself. She is standing outside the play, marking the disaster, and possibly moving more directly into a position to mourn. She insists to herself that she write it, in an attempt to gather herself for the work of grieving. Bishop has moved from denial of loss into the work—her writing process itself—that will move her further toward the integration of loss as reality. Her reality brings her to the reckoning that the breakdown has already occurred (Winnicott, 1971).

Her play has occurred through an engagement and manipulation of reality in fantasy and through language. She has created new rules and broken old rules. The old rule, foundational truth, is that loss is inevitable if we have lived and loved. Further, we don't have sovereignty over how we encounter loss in reality. Through her play with omnipotent fantasy, she has been able to integrate the reality of loss as disaster. Bishop is a kind of analyst to herself in her self-analysis as, through play, she has moved from denial and disavowal into trying to integrate reality. Grieving has occurred not only in her relationship to lost objects but also for the loss of a fantasy of power.

Case Vignettes

Rachael

Rachael was 30 years old when she began analysis. She said that she kept choosing unavailable men as partners. Rachael described her mother as an aggressive, full-time competitor for her father's attention. As our work unfolded, Rachael became more aware that her unlikely choices of men satisfied a particular fantasy in which she would select impossibly remote men with whom to find closeness. More available men could not be slotted for this internal fantasy of undoing her parent's impenetrable alliance; they barely registered on her radar.

Rachael and I came to understand that this repetition was not exclusively related to an Oedipal competition with her mother for her father's attention. She was also angry that her father felt that he had to submit to Rachael's mother's "every wish and desire." Rachael saw her mother as controlling and coercive and her father as weak for submitting to her mother's demands. Everything in the family seemed to revolve around her mother's infantile need to be the center of attention.

Shortly after beginning her treatment, Rachael began making a remark that I found humorous at the time, a remark that was to become a familiar refrain about going on dates with interesting and available men. She would say, "What fun is that?" She would say this when a man with whom she'd had fun on a first date would call her back and ask to see her again. "What fun is that?" she would ask, seemingly recognizing more fully the degree to which she had libidinized unavailable men.

These moments in which Rachael joked about her internalized fantasy of being with her unavailable father and with me were sometimes humorous and seemed to obviously involve a level of self-reflection about her renunciation and masochistic attachment to her father. Over time I realized that they belied a great deal of sadness about the way that she was wasting time that I was not fully recognizing. I began to feel a mild sense of irritation with Rachael's humor about her erotic masochism. I may have also been experiencing Rachael's disavowed sadness and anger and possibly a part of Rachael that sought revenge toward her mother through her symbolic adventures with patently unavailable men standing in for her father.

I began to translate a feeling, more like a concern, into a series of thoughts. I had worried that Rachael might make elements of analysis and my unavailability into another form of heroic activity in the transference for her to overcome. I began to think of the pronouncement, "What fun is that?" more as an idiomatic statement of her loyalty to me. It also seemed like the statement issued from a dissociated self-state in which I was supposed to go along with this form of dissociation. The "fun" that she was having related to using her analysis as a form of erotic masochism similar to what she had enacted with her many futile relationships. I was being recruited as an object of her desire that would go along with her forfeit of a real relationship. While this had likely occurred to me before, I am trying to highlight a moment in which my own experience of being inside this enactment was more pronounced. Specifically, I was noticing my own resistance to understanding Rachael's resistance to mourning the sense of feeling unseen by her parents and alone in her desires.

In her self-deprecating remark about erotic masochism as "fun," she reversed the rules of the game. In this rule change, not actually having a man is the fun and her mother's victory is the loss. I was implicitly going along with this rule change through a kind of superficial recognition of its meaning without understanding Rachael's resistance and my own to observing it as a form of play in the service of mourning.

In this developing realization, I was able to tell Rachael that I had stopped finding her joke funny and that I could better feel her anger and renunciation. I was now trying to change the rules of play myself or, more likely, I was responding to subtle changes in Rachael that I could not really identify or articulate even now. Rachael was able to take this in fairly easily which is partly why I say that she may have been quite close to knowing this herself. In other words, with Rachael and many other patients with whom I've worked, these kinds of changes in my countertransference awareness are often inter-subjectively related to changes that are underway in the patient's awareness as well.

My own resistance probably resided in a conscious and un-conscious enjoyment of Rachael's attachment to me. I was knowing but not feeling how much of Rachael's resistance revolved around substituting me along with the other men for her unavailable father. And I could reside with her in her dissociated states that matched with a version of dissociation on my part. For the first time, I un-derstood or at least more deeply felt that her remark was a form of play, not only about her repetition with men and how much it was linked to an unconscious partnership with her unavailable father, but also about entering into this relationship with me in the transference.

While I knew that Rachael was always being sarcastic in her re-mark, I had failed to see it as an attempt to mourn. "What fun" is a way of saying that it's sad to mourn and leave a compensatory so-lution, no matter how inadequate that solution has been. Inside her joke is an attempt to acknowledge that there is no fun in mourning her fantasy of substituting intercourse with unavailable men for her father. My developing awareness of irritability with Rachael's self-effacing humor allowed me to more actively confront her insistence on not mourning. I began to understand that she was introducing play into the transference as a protean way of grieving the loss of the "fun" (that was really not much fun at all and actually quite painful with her father) into a more direct playground with me in analysis.

Julie

Julie's very being was shaken when her sense of reality clashed with her parents' sense of reality. She felt dysregulated and consciously thought that she was being disloyal. She would sometimes cleave to her parents' views of reality rather than her own in order to secure her attachment to them.

Twenty-six years old when she began analysis, Julie was an accomplished graduate student when she began analysis, but she recalled having experienced these conflicts from early in her childhood. Her parents held views on many elements of reality that were disappointing to Julie, particularly in the areas of politics and religion but also in their practical advice. When her teachers in her graduate program would say something that was factually wrong about her area of expertise or simply get something wrong about the logistics of her graduate program requirements, she would feel quite anxious and destabilized. At these moments she felt it difficult to think and to trust herself.

We began to understand that in order to preserve an object relationship with the person who gets it wrong she had to view herself as the person who gets it wrong. She wanted to get it right and trust her own reality but attempting to do so left her feeling alone.

There were events that transpired between us in which she was shaken by perceptions that differed with mine. Sometimes I would barely complete my thought before she would agree. Over time I was able to gently take this up in the transference and she described feeling sad and lonely about our separateness, especially when she was able to give herself the space to reflect on what I had said. She enjoyed feeling that we saw things the same way even if it required her to create pseudo-agreement. She observed that she "rushed" to feel the connection with me rather than allow her own views to emerge. We also began to understand her wishes that I would know what she wanted or felt without her having to say.

Our examination of these processes was catalyzed by an error that I made in billing, one that favored her in terms of charging too little. Despite her wishes to please me by making a correction to my bill that would allow me to be paid the correct amount, she was destabilized by her feeling of conflict and high anxiety about having to report an error. Julie said that a part of her could not really believe that she was right, and I was wrong.

She associated to the familiar Cukor film, "Gaslight," a story about a man who is trying to drive his wife mad by constantly undermining her sense of reality. Julie said, "But you're not the one undermining my reality. I just feel like it's you making me crazy but it's me." I said, hoping not to be glib but feeling that what I was saying was important: "I am perhaps trying to undermine your sense of reality, your inner reality that requires you to acclimate to me. It is making you anxious." I was trying to help her trust her thoughts and feeling which was at odds with her wishes to acclimate to me. I had taken the rug out from under her.

When I spoke, I felt a kind of mild dysregulation, a barely noticeable wish to disrupt how compliantly locked in Julie was both to me in the transference and with her parents. We had been "playing nice" with each other. Julie had been often reflexively agreeing with me and I had been feeling an affectionate link to Julie's forced sense of needing to accommodate to her parents. I was also likely experiencing some of Julie's anger toward her parents that she was unable to feel, a form of projective identification. I had been trying to contain that set of feelings. We had arrived at a moment in which we were both less able to contain certain kinds of affects with one another.

Julie introduces play through the metaphor of gaslighting. Her paradoxical, idiomatic expression of gaslighting reverses my attempt to support her reality (regarding financial matters between us) and transforms it into a disruption of her equanimity. She brings us inside the place where disruption resides in her unconscious attachment to an internal object that requires compliance. An obscure rule of our transference-countertransference engagement involved the idea that if I facilitated too much her ability to trust her own mind, she unconsciously construed it as persecutory. If she was required to act on her own behalf, she would be challenging her family's "corporate motto" (Symington, 1983, p. 287) that had required her to agree with everything her parents said. Julie takes us inside that corporate motto where we find our own corporate motto with each other at the point of play, a prerequisite for the possibility of mourning and change.

It was also, I believe, the first time that Julie had sustained a negative or suspicious feeling toward me. I say, "I believe" because I cannot be certain whether it was the first time that her displeasure with me was expressed or simply the first time that it had registered for me as so vividly. She introduces a persecutory feeling or fantasy in which she is being manipulated again in a sense by me and her parents. In this new point of play, there are new rules for examining her unconscious attachment to an internal object whom she feels is controlling her. I enter into Julie's new rules of play. She says that I am gaslighting her and I agree. We are together in a new moment of understanding her terror of being dislodged from her compliance and from the minimization of parts of her experience.

While I cannot prove it, I wonder too if in my acknowledging my own wishes to gaslight Marianne (i.e. subvert her attachment to her parents), she might have unconsciously linked this acknowledgment to the ways that she had always been indoctrinated by her parents. Was I unconsciously trying on a form of acceptance of responsibility for this indoctrination as a parental admission, in absentia? Maybe too, in play there are new ways that roles are changing, and we try on new roles with one another in the analytic situation.

In this acceptance of responsibility for my role, "I am gaslighting you," in Benjamin's terms, through this recognition of the patient's protest, the repetition is transformed into repair of the patient's capacity for active assertion, for thinking and "meta-commentary" (Benjamin, 2016). Recognition that includes one's own reaction allows both partners to move from the desultory repetition of doer and done to. Benjamin (2004, 2016) has defined the moral position in which violations are acknowledged, and it is the precondition to the possibility for mourning. Julie and I have reached a new level of differentiation between each person's separate perspective or experience. In a sense, Julie's melancholic identification with her parents is now better able to be mourned.

The question of how we in Benjamin's terms, meta-communicate without appearing to invalidate one side is related to how we play by affirming with marking, by finding the Yes/And position. Play describes one method of developing the third space of paradox, acknowledging what feels real to the patient, while speaking from a potential place of overlap and difference. Benjamin (2016) states that "at times, of course, this occurs first by enacting the collision and sometimes this at least this gets the feared repetition out in the open. At other moments, through play we more gradually move the enactment into a space of collaboration without collision. We try to reshape the impasse by speaking from «inside» the play, as we lend ourselves and play our assigned role. We *perform* recognition rather than merely verbalize it, using marking to evoke a degree of difference. This is what it means to use our subjective expression to improvise, to introduce play within the enactment, to shift self-state so as to repair disruption or open up to emergent meanings of what is going on" (p. 565).

Julie and I spoke to each other in the "ventilated space" (Green, 1975) that resides slightly outside her unconscious need to hold on to an object tie that was debilitating but had felt necessary for her sense of attachment. This ventilated space also required me to dislodge myself from an unwitting overemphasis on understanding her need to acclimate to others. In doing so, I could take responsibility for my participation in facilitating her separation from both this position and the accompanying internal object attachments. Several sessions later as we integrated some of these developments, I was able to speak to Julie about her persecutory fantasy of what I was doing to her as an unconscious fantasy about how she would be devastating her parents—in fact persecuting them through her greater ability to separate.

Julie and I continued to understand how her sense of her self-abnegation preserved an unconscious fantasy of her parents as all-knowing caretakers. Julie slowly developed a sense of being supported for thinking in ways that were independent from her parents and from me. She became better able to distinguish between a burgeoning sense of self (one that left her alone) versus a selfless feeling of survival, one that had been supported by her forced belief in the omnipotence of others. Julie became better able to feel alone in my presence in the transference (Winnicott, 1958), a paradoxical experience of self with other that honored listening to what her mind spoke. She became aware of grief about feeling that she had never had this experience with her parents.

Discussion: Mourning and the Ethics of Play

Playing serves to help patients move toward grieving internal objects. This play often occurs in the density of psychic regression and progression. The part of the ego that has been linked to or identified with the internal object (Freud, 1917) is now slowly replaced with parts of self that can observe the internal object in a different developmental context that originally gave rise to the internalization. The patient can observe this internalized object in more frankly wasteful terms within the holding environment of analysis, a setting in which the analyst appreciates the patient's artful, adaptive afflictions that were used to survive. In fact, the analyst's appreciation of the patient's adaptations is often a form of play when it can be appreciated, seriously and with compassion, for the conditions that required its creation. Along these lines, Coen (2005) has illustrated quite beautifully some of the ways that the analyst needs to connect to the remote patient's protective core.

The patient's sense of psychic forfeit is held in a transference-countertransference context in a new way. The patient is better able to acquire an "internal environment" (Winnicott, 1945), one in which the ego can hold separateness. In these moments, patients can better face the profound disappointment of grieving these objects. A point of play is reached within experiences of intersubjective engagement that shed light on the loss and waste that has also been enacted in transference-countertransference engagement.

Vygotsky's notion of how imaginative play helps children to develop meaning and make sense of the reality in which they live may provide further help in considering the relationship of play and mourning. With imaginative play, children often engage in pretend role-playing activities involving dialogues that they develop with other children. It also involves exercising problem-solving skills as they work out the plot of their story: what their characters are going to do or how they will defeat the villain. The dialogues they create help them to develop their language as they imitate things that they have observed in the real world. Even when children engage in imaginative play by themselves, they engage in these dialogues with themselves that help them to develop language and problem-solving skills. Vygotsky believed that the external language that children hear and imitate is internalized during imaginative play. In a sense, play is being used by the child in development to practice play and integrating reality.

As I emphasized in Chapter 3, limit is constitutive of play. Thus the rule-bound foundations of play that Vygotsky stressed are likely to assist in mourning the loss of unconscious fantasy (e.g. a fantasy of complete freedom to make up rules). Imaginative play is always juxtaposed against a reality that exists outside the changing of rules that facilitate play. Winnicott wrote of "playing and reality" in contrast to the notion of "playing versus reality." The adult, attached to problematic internal objects, learns to play with what constitutes new rules. Play may permit a new view or appreciation of the toxic or binding nature of the attachment. In the new rules, their fantasies of holding on to internalized object relations may be challenged, opening up a new way to integrate mourning with play rather than suffer with the deprivation of limit.

In the clinical examples here, play is introduced by the analytic couple in the service of grieving. Patient and analyst work with a form of play in which interpretations are experienced paradoxically. For example, Julie felt disrupted, even undermined by my affirmation of her own, accurate observations. She felt this way because her own mind and my mind were like rogue agents acting outside her unconscious pact to be in a fused relational experience with her parents, even at the cost of her sense of reality and selfhood.

Julie could feel the regressive pull to join with her parents' reality even in the face of experiencing herself as needing to retreat from her own thoughts and feelings. In a moment in which play was reached, we realized that I had all along inhabited her alarming thought that I was trying to undermine her reality. Her fantasy was in fact in some way true but hidden in plain sight in terms of what we were doing together. As the helpful regressive experience of analysis unfolded, Julie began to feel that her separateness from her parents, as well as my separateness from her, was persecutory. I could better experience and understand levels of enactment in which I had not confronted her terror of separation as well as her protean attempts to mourn. At the moment of play, Julie could feel more strongly her terror of aloneness without her parents if she was to let herself trust her own mind and mine. She also located her fear of hurting her parents through her separateness. Julie became better able in the transference to feel my support for her mind, one that provided greater separation from her internal punitive objects.

Some of these clinical examples of patients and analysts finding play in relation to the objects with whom the patient has felt tyrannized raise questions about the blurry distinctions between self-deprecating humor about their pathology, emergent self-observation, and play. I would suggest that sometimes play, in contrast to self-reproach, is more characterized by a relational experience with the analyst in which the patient's problems, their attachments to old objects and experience, are brought into the transference and held with compassion and appreciation. Humor involves laughing with the self and analyst rather than laughing at when the movement toward mourning is in play. To be sure though, these are not always easy distinctions to make. Sometimes it is the small, seemingly repetitive detail in a form of familiar, idiomatic speech that cues us into a glimmer of play that I have emphasized. We know that play in the form of humor may sometimes involve a double-edged sword, both attacking oneself while trying to find parts of one's mind that are not tyrannized by unconscious, internal object relations.

In Chapter 2, I took up the matter of an ethic of play. When Winnicott (1945) suggested that the analyst is both a supervisor and participant in play, he was implying that it is the analyst who maintains the frame of analytic work. As I have noted, the ethics of play require us to keep our eye on the inevitable and constant emergence of enactments, since there is no way for play to exist outside transference-countertransference enactment. Among the guardrails to keep in mind involves the potential to side with the persecutory parts of the patient that can use analytic understandings as a further form of self-recrimination. Self-effacing humor or humor directed toward the patient that is in the service of degrading the patient can often occur in ways that are less noticeable than we might think. Rachael's humor about the lack of "fun" that she experienced with available men was self-effacing, but it was, I discovered, eventually grounded in a much richer transference-countertransference setting. Interestingly, a kind of signal anxiety operated when I began to feel that Rachael's question, "what fun is that?" was a form of erotic masochism that she was seeking to institutionalize in the analysis like she had in her outside life. My experience in the countertransference with Rachael was one in which I felt that she was bringing herself into the present, enjoying the ways that I was available to her. This holding allowed her greater distance from the catastrophe that had already occurred in her childhood.

Since in play, rules are made up as the participants go along, an ethic of play involves the reality also that certain extant rules will be changed as we go along. There are ethical rules that cannot be broken under any circumstances. In psychoanalysis we create a new rule (sort of) by encouraging patients to say what comes to mind, breaking conventional rules of expressive constraint. Laplanche (1987) suggested that psychoanalysis invites us into a "primal seduction to describe a fundamental situation in which an adult proffers to a child, verbal, non-verbal, and even behavioral signifiers which are pregnant with sexual unconscious signification" (p. 126). Wilson (2006, 2013) suggests that it is inherent in the ethical context of psychoanalysis that the analyst leave unadorned and unprotected both his desire and lack.

One of the most important countertransference activities (Wilson, 2013) for the analyst in helping to bring patients to points of play resides in our ability to find ventilated spaces of our own in relation to transference-countertransference. This is another dimension of the ethic of play. It is also fair to say that as Morris (2016, p. 1184) suggests, "analyst and analysand must both survive the primal seduction of the other in order for analysis to ethically happen." In a transition to mourning, the play that I described with Nina involved embracing this risk and changing the previous rules of our transference-countertransference engagement.

Elizabeth Bishop's play in "One Art" takes on a few forms of humor. She is sarcastically minimizing some of the disasters she has experienced related to loss. Bishop works up to an ability to exist in present time as she completes her poem and takes in the present experience of loss as disaster. Her use of sarcasm could be seen as simultaneously involving defenses against the experience of loss while providing a form of self-soothing and holding about adapting to inevitable loss. Her defenses function as "double agents" (Schafer, 1968) both minimizing expressiveness and at the same time allowing the impulse to break through. She is trying to imagine a new possible integration of grief as a kind of analyst to herself, even as she is trying to mitigate her experiences of loss (Cooper, 1997; Griffin, 2020).

Play requires us to continually monitor our countertransference as outsider to the patient's internal world. These requirements are so arduous and precarious because if we are to find points of play, we will inevitably be drawn into the patient's inner persecutory world. This sobering awareness reminds us that in play, even as newness emerges, its persecutory potential (e.g. being played by another) is always an exacting and enlivening risk. Through newly discovered forms of play, including risk, these processes are occurring now in real time and less through frozen memorialization of what never was.

References

Benjamin, J. (2004) Beyond doer and done to: An intersubjective view of thirdness. *Psychoanal. Quarter.* 73(1): 5–46. 10.1002/j.2167-4086.2004.tb00151.x

Benjamin, J. (2016) From enactment to play: Metacommunication, acknowledgement, and the third of paradox. *Rivista di Psychoanalisi* 62: 565–593.

Bishop, E. (1994) *One Art*. New York: Ferrer, Strauss, & Giroux.

Coen, S. J. (2005) How to play with patients who would rather remain remote. *J. Amer. Psychoanal. Assn.* 53: 811–834.

Cooper, S. H. (1997) Interpretation and the psychic future. *Int. J. Psycho-Anal.* 78: 667–681.

Cooper, S. H. (2010) The analyst's anticipatory fantasies: Aid and obstacle to the patient's self-integration. *Psychoanal. Dial.* 20(4): 459–474.

Cooper, S. H. (2015) Reflections on the analyst's "good enough" capacity to bear disappointment, with special attention to repetition. *J. Amer. Psychoanal. Assn.* 63(6):1193–1213.

Cooper, S. H. (2018) Playing in the darkness: Use of the object and use of the subject. *J. Amer. Psychoanal. Assn.* 66(4): 743–765.

Cooper, S. H. (2019) A theory of the setting: The transformation of unrepresented experience and play. *Int. J. Psycho-Anal.* 100:1439–1454.

Cooper, S. H. (2021) Toward an ethic of play. *Psychoanal. Q.* 90(3): 371–390.

Cooper, S. H. (in press) The limit of intimacy and the intimacy of limit: Play and its relation to the bad object. *J. Amer. Psychoanal. Assn.*

Davies, J. M. (2004) Whose bad objects are we anyway? Repetition and our elusive love affair with evil. *Psychoanal. Dial.* 14: 711–732.

Fairbairn, R. (1952) *Psychoanalytic Studies of the Personality*. London: Tavistock Publications.

Freud, S. (1914) Remembering, repeating, and working through. *S.E.* 12: 145–156.

Freud, S. (1917) Mourning and melancholia. *S.E.* 14: 237–258.

Green, A. (1975) The analyst, symbolization, and absence in the analytic setting – in memory of D. W. Winnicott. *Int. J. Psycho-Anal.* 56: 9–22.

Green, A. (2008) *The Chains of Eros: The Sexual in Psychoanalysis*. London: Routledge.

Griffin, F. L. (2020) Becoming of use as an analyst: Imagining something that was never there before. *J. Amer. Psychoanal. Assn.* 68: 27–58.

Loewald, H. (1960) The therapeutic action. *Int. J. Psychoanal.* 41: 46–63.

Modell, A. M. (1975) On having the right to a life: An aspect of the superego's development. *Int. J. Psycho-Anal.* 46: 223–231.

Ogden, T. (1989) On the concept of the autistic-contiguous position. *Int. J. Psycho-Anal.* 70: 127–140.

Ogden, T. (2010) Why read Fairbairn. *Int. J. Psycho-Anal.* 91: 101–118.

Ogden, T. (2012) *Creative Readings: Essays on Seminal Works.* London: New Library of Psychoanalysis.

Parsons, M. (1999) The logic of play in psychoanalysis. *Int. J. Psycho-Anal.* 80(5): 871–884.

Parsons, M. (2009) An independent theory of clinical technique. *Psychoanal. Dial.* 19: 221–236.

Pizer, S. A. (1996) The negotiation of paradox in the analytic process. *Psychoanal. Dial.* 2: 215–240.

Ringstrom, P. A. (2001) Cultivating the improvisational in psychoanalytic treatment. *Psychoanal. Dial.* 11(5): 727–754.

Schafer, R. (1968) The mechanisms of defense. *Int. J. Psycho-Anal.* 49: 49–62.

Symington, N. (1983) The analyst's act of freedom as agent of therapeutic change. *Int. Rev. Psychoanal.* 10: 283–291.

Vygotsky, L. (1934/2012) *Thought and Language.* Cambridge: MIT Press.

Wilson, M. (2013) Desire and responsibility: The ethics of countertransference experience. *Psychoanal. Q.* 82: 435–476.

Winnicott, D. W. (1945) Primitive emotional development. In: *Through Paediatrics in Psychoanalysis* (pp. 145–156). New York: Basic Books.

Winnicott, D. W. (1949) Hate in the countertransference. In: *Through Paediatrics in Psychoanalysis* (pp. 194–203). New York: Basic Books.

Winnicott, D. W. (1951) Transitional objects and transitional phenomena. In: *Playing ad Reality* (pp. 1–25). New York: Basic Books.

Winnicott, D. W. (1958) The capacity to be alone. *Int. J. Psycho-Anal.* 39: 416–420.

Winnicott, D. W. (1968) Playing: Its theoretical status in the clinical situation. *Int. J. Psycho-Anal.* 49: 591–599.

Winnicott, D. W. (1969) The use of an object. *Int. J. Psycho-Anal.* 50: 711–716.

Winnicott, D. W. (1974) Fear of breakdown. *Int. R. Psycho-Anal.* 1: 103–107.

Wittgenstein, L. (1953) *Philosophical Investigations.* New York: MacMillan Publishing Company.

Chapter 5

A Theory of the Setting: The Transformation of Unrepresented Experience and Play [1]

I wrote parts of this chapter as a plenary address for the Centenary Celebration of the *International Journal of Psychoanalysis*. I chose to focus on the concept of the setting because it is central to how we create a home for the emergence of and language for unrepresented experience.

In the evolution of psychoanalytic theory, the setting concept reflected the need to explore both the material arrangements and the psychic dimensions of the psychoanalytic process. The concept of the setting emerged as a metaphoric structure to conceptualize the links between objects, particularly between patient and analyst. As Field Theory and the theories of Bion and Winnicott emerged, Kleinian theory further expanded, and new theoretical developments in North America took hold, psychoanalysis needed a metaphoric ecology, a third space, to hold both the separate and intertwined subjectivities of patient and analyst. We needed to conceptualize not only the transference-countertransference relationship but also the affective and ideational matrix in which the transference-countertransference is generated and understood by patient and analyst (Ogden, 1991). Laplanche indirectly made an essential and similar point about the setting in 1999 when he stated: "On the whole, we have moved from the analysis of transference to analysis situated in transference."

Here, I offer some observations toward a personal theory of the setting, one that is influenced especially by Winnicott, and also Bleger (1967a, b), Modell (1976; 1989) and Ogden (2004a). I will develop and interweave two central themes through some brief clinical vignettes. The first is that the setting houses the transition from unrepresented to

DOI: 10.4324/9781003265078-6

represented experience. The second relates to how the setting is a location of dynamic transit between the vital, interactive elements of containment and interpretation of the patient's unconscious and conscious experience. Process and non-process elements of the setting are always interacting with one another, an observation made also by Quinodoz (1992) and Brown (2015). The setting operates as an auxiliary function for the analyst's capacities, which include containment, interpretation, and as a "participant and supervisor of play" (Winnicott, 1968).

One of the most important functions of the setting is to mark the way that analytic play is organized. Play often juxtaposes the patient's new fantasied rules with those rules that the analyst provides regarding the setting, those that make psychoanalysis possible. Often play occurs in relationship to the patient's attempt to subvert or undo rules, especially those that prevent sexual and emotional gratification. In this way play communicates unconscious phantasy and the tensions between the setting as a real object/place and one that owes its existence to the patient's internal fantasy life.

A Brief Review of the Setting Concept

I view Winnicott as our most important setting theorist since Freud. Winnicott identified dual elements of object function in the setting: His work on charting "normal" developmental processes; theorizing the importance of illusion and play in relationship to integrating reality; and his many contributions to understanding trauma and severe personality disorder have overshadowed his attempts to delineate the dual elements of holding and interpretation in the setting.

Winnicott's redefinition of the analytic process in terms of play is related to his view of the setting. Play provides a link between unsymbolized experience and greater capacities for representation. In other words, for Winnicott the concept of play evolved as one of the ways that the analyst translates and meets the patient's offering of unconscious and unrepresented experience. In a sense Winnicott emphasized play as what translates Freud's (1914) groundbreaking observation that the unconscious must be enacted before it can be expressed. Thus, Winnicott's decision to feature play as central to therapeutic action was responsive to Freud's delineation of the vexing problem of how we go about translating unconscious into conscious experience.

Winnicott suggests that as a supervisor of play, the analyst creates some of the rules of analytic play that will become the basis of projection, illusion, transference, and interpretation. The environment mother holds responsibility for fixed analytic arrangements that include the supervision of play. In this chapter, I hope to elaborate the connection between the setting and object relationship as well as the links between play and understanding unrepresented experience.

Bleger's (1967a, b) influential understanding of the setting included Winnicott's notion of the facilitating environment but also related to a few different transitions in psychoanalytic thinking. He provided a metaphoric container for grasping the transit between psychotic and non-psychotic parts of the personality in clinical process. His clinical understanding of how unconscious fantasies are enacted in the setting was also a very early and deeply insightful view of enactment between patient and analyst, including the inevitability of the analyst's blind spots. Steiner (2006) elaborated on Bleger's work on the inevitability of the patient and analyst's verbal and behavioral countertransference enactments in relationship to the setting.

For Bleger (1967) the setting constitutes a silent base, a constant permitting of the variables of the process to emerge. Green (1975) explicitly sought to extend Bleger when he stated (p. 8).

To clarify things we can say that the analytic situation is the totality of the elements making up the analytic relationship, at the heart of which we can, in the course of time, observe a process whose knots are tied by the transference and the countertransference, due to the establishment and the limits of the analytic setting. This definition completes that given by Bleger (1967a).

Ogden's rich body of work describing the psychoanalytic process does not explicitly address the setting as a separate topic. Instead though, Ogden's (2004a) descriptions of the dynamic relationship between container/contained and holding as well as the fluid relationship between the autistic-contiguous, paranoid-schizoid, and depressive positions (Ogden, 1991) provide ways of thinking of the setting as the container for expression of unconscious fantasy from both patient and analyst.

Modell (1989) emphasized that the simultaneous communication between the symbolic actualization of early parenting in the analytic setting and higher level, more developed parts of the patient is a unique characteristic of the analytic setting. In this sense, Modell (1989) suggested that the setting holds the paradox of regression and growth, one that is held by the analyst's capacities to observe multiple levels of reality.

I suggest that while the analyst provides a setting that is fixed with regard to issues of time, place and explicit rules governing the analytic situation, a very important dimension of the setting is co-created by the patient and analyst. In recent years, analysts from different theoretical perspectives have been trying to elaborate their own views on how the setting is co-created between patient and analyst (e.g. Bass, 2007; Goldberg, 1989; Parsons, 2007).

The setting is partially co-created through collisions between the external setting and the patient's conscious and unconscious fantasies about the setting. Despite the patient's need to repeat and to find earlier, internalized object relationships, what is not fixed is the contemporary object relation within the setting. Seen from this perspective, the setting may be seen as in part a fantasy, or piece of mental life, made up, like all other such pieces, of defenses and unconscious fantasies including wishes and self-punishments (e.g. Brenner, 1979). Thus, tensions between stability and instability in the setting derive from three sources: the relative proportion of symbolized versus unsymbolized elements, the continual enactments between patient and analyst hidden in full view, and the collisions between the fixed extrinsic elements of the setting and the fantasies within the patient's and analyst's internal settings.

I hope to develop an understanding of the setting as not just a set of rules of engagement that facilitate the analytic process but something that is itself incorporated into that process. The setting is a set of rules of engagement that facilitate the finding of unconscious content through interaction between the intrinsically regressive elements of the analytic situation and the unique intersubjective context in any analytic dyad.

I emphasize that the setting also marks the *limits of representation*, the enigmatic depth of all psychic production and messaging. As we know, all psychic production intrinsically eludes or is outside what is representable. Pontalis (1997) writes, "The reality of psychoanalysis can only reside at the limits of the analyzable." Part of what the setting is instituting then is the development of a culture, belief system, and history of the *limits of representation*. The setting is also instituting a history of the analytic couple's efforts to work with the emergence of representation, including the conflict between expressiveness and restraint.

This view of the setting as a culture representing the limits of representation seems to me to be an elaboration of Winnicott's view of interpretation itself as a marker of the analyst's understanding. The setting facilitates understanding and representation as a holder of the patient and of the limits of what patient and analyst can find and contain together.

The Objects in the Setting and the Setting in the Object

Analysts differ in whether they see the setting as a separate structure from the central object relation within it. Bleger (1967a, b) delineated that the setting consists of an enduring structure that holds a set of norms and attitudes. This structure is by definition an institution, one that receives especially the undifferentiated and non-solved aspects of the patient's primitive symbiotic links. Winnicott suggested that the object relation itself performs several functions: one related to holding and attachment functions and the management of the setting, and the other an object that receives affects, instincts, and transference.

For Segal (1962) the setting was seen as essential in the development of transference. She stated (1962, pp. 212–213) we undertake that the analyst shall do nothing to blur the development of the transference, that he shall be there as a person whose sole function is to understand sympathetically and to communicate to the patient such relevant knowledge as he has acquired at the moment when the analysand is most ready to understand it.

Since Segal (e.g. Bleger, 1967a; Steiner, 2006) numerous analysts have accepted that the best we can do is to try to understand how analysts do things unconsciously to interfere with these conditions of the setting.

In my view of the setting, the recurrent elements of the physical arrangement of psychoanalysis that encourage regression are an

extension of each of the analyst's functions as container and transference object. The qualities of the patient's and analyst's internal
objects along with the recurrent material elements of the setting are
what are institutionalized within the analytic couple. Thus, I conceptualize the setting as part of the transference-countertransference
matrix, just as it holds elements of the transference. Analysis is set in
the milieu of transference (Laplanche, 1999). This means that unfortunately, we can even anticipate that the establishment of the
setting, despite our best efforts, may enact elements of the patient's
and analyst's unconscious experience that jeopardize understanding.

At the core of the analytic setting is the unique blend of ritualized,
asymmetrical, and spontaneous parts of the analytic relationship that
comprises the "as if" structure of analytic process, the "rules of the
game" that Huizinga (1932) described as a part of all forms of play.
Regarding the rules of the game, Green (1975) emphasized that the
analytic subject is born in intersubjective space, from the separate
individual subjectivities of patient and analyst. It can only germinate
in the elements of the setting that involve limit.

In concert with the particularities of the patient's and analyst's
sensibilities, in the patient's mind the recurring and constant aspects
of the physical characteristics of the setting are experienced as a
quality of the analytic relationship. The psychoanalytic setting is
uniquely capable of providing flooring for symbolization and what
Modell (1989, p. 5) referred to as "symbolic actualization" of early
developmental experiences. These symbolic transformations are at
their essence forms of transference, stimulated by the setting as an
artificially constructed space in which fantasy, drives and their deri-
vatives can be brought into play through speech. The setting holds
the patient's regression just as it stimulates or incites it.

The object tie to the analyst is, as Freud (1915) suggested, fundamentally paradoxical in that the analysand's love for and dependency
on the analyst occurs within a different level of reality (Modell, 1989):
the psychoanalytic setting. For Winnicott, the rules that govern the
setting are a form of containment of that space, essential in their
functions as a preserve for illusion. Building on Winnicott, I would
add that the setting as a containment of that space is like analytic love
and dependency itself, both real and illusory. The most enigmatic,
unfamiliar elements of the patients' and analysts' minds are to some

extent out of reach to both themselves and the other, leading to the inevitability of enactments.

While the most institutionalized elements of the setting influence patient and analyst, at the same time, the characteristics and history of the intersubjective field also shape what is institutionalized. For example, the unique sensibilities of the patient and analyst, including their internal objects, conflicts, and defenses, determine what is concordant and discordant between them and thus also shape and cloak that environment. This has been emphasized by Feldman (1997) among many others within the Kleinian literature and Greenberg (1995) within the interpersonal literature. I observed in an earlier paper (Cooper, 2009; 2010 also see Lafarge, 2018) that patients and analysts form a historical record or experience of the analyst's interpretive style that is part of what is lost and disrupted during termination. Perhaps this loss is similar to Lemma's (2014) observation that elements of the analyst's physical characteristics are also experienced as a loss during termination. The evolution of the setting is a function of the couple that, one could say, involves a process of "personalization," or, in Roussillon's terms, a subjectivation of the setting that is specific to that analytic pair. The setting borrows from that accrued experience, reinforced by the analyst's commitment to it, which in turn grounds it in an experience between the two participants.

Part of what is also institutionalized, then, entered into the history book of each analytic pair, are the transitions from raw, unrepresented experience to reflection and new metaphors within the analytic dyad. If we look at moments when we come close to understanding enactments within the setting, such as the patient's relationship to the time of appointments or a fee arrangement that had contained hidden meanings, we are always partly dependent on the particular and shifting elements of analytic concordance in the dyad that permit seeing and not seeing. This is another meaning to the notion that the setting is always in the process of being set or changing.

In the following brief vignettes, I highlight that patient and analyst have enacted some of the patient's unconscious fantasies in the creation of the setting (see also Steiner, 2006). These arrangements and the awareness of enactments are unique to particular elements of the patients and analyst's personalities and their particular intersubjective field. These examples put into focus how bastions in the setting are common, a point well illustrated by Bleger (1967a, b). Bastions may form around an overemphasis on the patient's either relatively easy or problematic acclimation to the setting.

Case Vignette I

Patient A has arranged a fee with her candidate analyst in training. She insisted on a fee that was close to the analyst's full fee. The analyst agreed to this fee and was grateful but feared that the fee might be too high for the patient. A was convinced that the fee was realistic. During the first several months of analysis, the patient described sometimes working long extra hours to pay her bills including her analytic fees. At times, the analyst silently wondered about whether A may have masochistically deprived herself of pleasure, maximizing hours of extra work in order to pay for her analysis, or created a sense of guilty suffering in the analyst for extracting too much from the patient. The likelihood of erotic sado-masochism had apparently flooded the setting.

Patient A and her analyst began to explore more and more the patient's identification with her father who worked long hours to help support the family. The patient viewed her mother as a spendthrift and experienced many unresolved hostile and competitive feelings toward her mother. She consciously wished to be much more like her father than her mother and fantasized that she would have been a much more satisfying partner to her father. As this material emerged, the patient and analyst were able to consider with much more breadth the concern around fee arrangements as a manifestation of Oedipal hostility and competitiveness toward her mother. As analysis unfolded, the rules of play established by the patient were revealed, reflecting the patient's unconscious and conscious attempt to create a setting that would buttress her anti-identification with her mother and gratify an Oedipal fantasy of union with her father. The analyst was recruited to play out this scenario as a maternal spendthrift—a selfish and greedy mother—by accepting the fee, rather than to help the patient become more reflective about her intense hostility and competitiveness with her mother and frustrated longings toward her father.

For this patient, the setting held some of her most disturbing feelings of hostility and competition toward her mother as well as some ways that she indirectly secured Oedipal gratification. The patient and analyst were able to better understand these enactments of an early pattern of object relation in the setting when the patient was able to articulate the emergent element of erotic masochism involved in perpetuating Oedipal fantasies. In Bleger (1967a, b) terms, we might say that the setting began to "weep."

With regard to how we view the setting, it is noteworthy that different analysts create a setting or grasp its weeping through enactments at different times and in different ways with each of their patients based on their own self-reflective capacities, their relationship to others and the history of their institutionalized relationship to psychoanalysis.

Case Vignette 2

Here is another example of the ways in which the objects in the setting each collide with the setting as an object. J is a highly successful, married entrepreneur in his late 50s who had recently ended a three-month analysis with a female colleague, which required a much longer commute than my office did. He and his analyst reluctantly agreed to stop analysis due to what was described as J's frequent travel and scheduling conflicts. According to J, they decided that the process might be more effective if J worked with an analyst located in the area in which he worked and lived. While J and his analyst felt that his schedule was not conducive to the analysis, each suspected that other elements of the analysis were not yet so well understood.

J was two years younger than his sister, who like him had been a highly successful student. J had felt that his mother was closer to his sister and that his sister and mother were often competitive with him for attention of J's father. J's mother had idolized her father, who died when she was nine years old. She fell in love with her 15-year-older husband when she was in her early 30s and maintained an apparent deep idealization of him until J's parents divorced when he was 15 years old. According to J, his mother felt threatened by her husband's fascination with J's sister and to a lesser extent with him. This was especially apparent in second grade, when he recalled that his sister began receiving increasing amounts of general attention for her intellectual abilities. J was envious of his sister.

In his current life, to the extent that he was highly successful in his work and powerful in his transactions with others, he felt that his wife of 25 years was excited and admiring but he held a fear and even dread that she was repulsed by his dependency needs and fears of abandonment. Fifteen years earlier when the patient's first business venture had failed, he felt that his wife was impatient with him and less supportive than he wished. Nevertheless, even at the beginning of his analysis, he linked some of these feelings toward his wife with his sense that his mother didn't welcome his anxieties and needs. J had been unable to ask his wife for more acknowledgment because he said that she was disappointed when he asked. J said that his wife felt that he was being controlling and coercive in the asking, some of which he agreed was true. J's wife maintained that just because she didn't always agree with what he wanted or wasn't as responsive to his anxiety as he wished, she didn't feel rejecting of him. To some extent, J was able to see his wife's side of things. In the countertransference, I was finding perspective of J's wife compatible with the idea that J was projecting on to his wife some of the sadness and anxiety that he had felt with his mother.

In the particular hour that I summarize within the first few months of analysis, he described feeling that he had organized a social event related to his business associates and potential new clients at his home and had wanted to make the decisions. He also dreaded a conflict with his wife because she resented how controlling she felt he could be during such events. He said that from his perspective his wife became angry prior to the event because she had been on the surface invited to plan but in reality, excluded from planning. J's wife felt that he had covered this up by what she viewed as "his phony request for her participation." She also felt micromanaged at the event. He blurted out in his session, "Why didn't she understand that I was anxious about having a good party? They never understand that I'm anxious." He associated to how his wife had thought that he wanted to be in control of the planning but pretended to include her and "did some phony, pseudo feminist bullshit pretend talk." According to J, by this she meant that she could have input, but that J wouldn't actually implement it unless it was in line with what he wanted. He said, "She loves the way I am in control at work and in bed with her but when I'm anxious she doesn't like my forcefulness, so I cover it up. I think that the covering up, the dissembling is what annoys her."

I wondered aloud whether J's wife was supposed to understand without his words that he felt anxious about saying how much he wanted things to be a certain way. J said that he felt that his mother was never interested in knowing what he was worried about and that he had to cover up his anxiety and needs to be seen as well as his needs to influence and have power because she was preoccupied or threatened.

As we explored these matters over several sessions, we began to talk about the same dynamic with his arrangements with his earlier analyst. He had chosen inconvenience from the beginning and acted out his sense of being put out, covertly hiding his self-interest and desires. I told him that he wanted his wife to understand that he had felt himself to be anxious, sadly isolated, and misunderstood about the party. This mirrored his feeling that he had to be a strong little boy in order to win his mother's favor but at times he wanted her to know that he was sad and needed help. We were all to understand, without him saying, both that he wanted what he wanted and that he needed to hide in order to preserve his tie to us. In a sense, his former analyst was recruited to play the part of a mother who wished for him to make things happen even though he was concealing his anxiety and anger about logistic matters related to analysis.

J had created and attacked the setting as an object, forcing it to be what he wished it to be—a construction that he creates in his wish to control others and events as well as his wish to be understood as a little boy frightened of abandonment. He agreed that in his fantasy, my location—which was a short commute from his work—would provide a seamless fit with his own early wishes to be validated and seen. Our setting began as a container for the unresolved weeping and un-analyzed collisions with the earlier setting while requiring us to con-sider its repetition in new forms within this setting. Not surprisingly, this pattern began to emerge quite prominently in relation to his wish that I provide him with special arrangements for his travel schedule.

As was true for the first vignette, there is a constant interaction between the stability of the provided setting and the patient's libidinally and aggressively tinged ways of making the setting coalesce to his or her internal settings. The unique sensibilities of the analyst will render him more or less attuned to the ways that his patient works with the provided setting. The analyst's preservation of his own sense of the setting and reality is essential in understanding enactments when they do occur.

Play at the Seam between Unrepresented and Represented Experience

The setting contains and stands at the porous border between the unrepresented/somatic/sensory and the more represented experience. Unconscious fantasy and play that are related to the setting often involve the transit between what is unrepresented and what is represented.

There is nearly always a tension between the setting as a real object and one that is organized by the patient's unconscious fantasies. Play often poses a contrast between the patient's new fantasied rules and the rules that the analyst provides regarding the setting. And it is the collision between the patient's rules and the analyst's rules that actually make analysis possible. Play is frequently organized around the patient's attempt to subvert or undo rules that prevent sexual and emotional gratification.

Some of the most important activities of play occur less inside symbolized elements of the analytic relationship and more on the outskirts of its yet unrealized possibility (Cooper, 2018). Green (1975) referred to a kind of seam between represented and unrepresented experience as "ventilated spaces." It is at these inflexion points, collision points between the patient's and analyst's internal settings for psychoanalysis, that the setting holds the analyst's attempts to find the patient's rules of play, rules whose meaning is defended against by the patient and sometimes inaccessible to the analyst as well.

Goldberg (1989, 2017, in press) has described many varieties of these collisions, focusing especially on the realm of psycho sensori/perceptual experience that the analyst needs to pay attention to, particularly with patients who have limited capacities for verbalizing thoughts and feelings. Goldberg directs us to incorporate a fundamental process of repairing or even establishing some more reliable "shared perceptual framework" between patient and analyst. While Goldberg's focus is not on play, the moments he describes in which analysts find their patients are often points of play.

A distinctive characteristic of the setting that facilitates play is its ability to hold elements of both fusion and separateness. In the most basic sense, the setting is that foundation of the analytic relationship that involves "the simultaneity of the dialectic of oneness and twoness, of individual subjectivity and intersubjectivity" (Ogden, 1994, p. 74n). The patient's and analyst's relationship to the setting is constantly, paradoxically, both separate and shared. Play is partly organized in the setting in relation to this paradox. Separateness is embedded in the limitations of the analytic relationship and the rules of analytic play. The manner in which sessions begin and end on time marks a kind of foundational separateness that exists on another level of reality than the symbiotic elements within the setting. The setting's holding of separateness is reflected in honoring the patient's and analyst's experience of unreachable, incommunicado parts of the self (Winnicott, 1963a).

Most patients, even those who have lacked ideal maternal holding (e.g. Green, 1997), are able to find some form of internal setting that can make use of the simultaneity of separation and fusion in the setting. However, for patients who have experienced high levels of parental neglect, the paradox of "both in this alone" (Bion, 1959), of the simultaneity of intimacy and solitude, is particularly challenging.

In the following clinical example, I describe a constant and painful collision between the setting as an offering by the analyst and the patient's conscious and unconscious fantasies about the analytic setting. Sometimes these collisions reveal unconsciously communicated protean capacities for play. I highlight a patient's struggles with a quality of aborted transit between the autistic-contiguous and paranoid-schizoid positions. This patient was eventually able to better symbolize elements of an autistic contiguous position and move from an unwieldy concrete insistence for physical contact to a more workable transference, albeit still related to the intense sexualization of early maternal longings. It might also help to illustrate the analyst's attempts to hold multiple levels of reality, including attention to forms of play at the seam between unrepresented and represented experience. When analytic work is successful, patients are able to feel more freedom to experience transit between their frustrations about the intrinsic limitations of the setting and the ability to make "use" (Winnicott, 1969) of the setting and the analytic process.

Clinical Vignette 1

Nina is a 30-year-old female scientist whom I described in Chapter 2. She is married to a woman and has had a history of frequent, brief sexual relationships with men and women before and since her three-year marriage. She is suffering with a sense of compulsively seducing women and men and then feeling quite empty after these experiences. Nina's wife wanted to have children while Nina was still quite uncertain about doing so. Nina states that she loves her wife but doesn't know what to do with her own constant need to be affirmed in terms of her attractiveness. She describes her sexual longings as an ache that cannot be fulfilled.

Nina began analysis with a fantasy that her previous psychotherapist had contacted me before I had met with her in order to warn me of her limitations. Nina and I understood that she would be starting our work together as the unwanted child she experienced herself to be with her neglectful parents, or, as I put it to her, "disappointing on arrival."

In the session that I summarize, a year into her four times a week analysis, Nina brings a recent photograph that she has taken of a roller coaster in ruin, a kind of relic from a period of time perhaps three or four decades before the present. She asks me to look at the photo as she lies down on the couch. She is quiet and I internally associate to the photo as a self-representation, an object similar in age to Nina. Nina then explains that she recently found this roller coaster in some traveling with her wife through rural New England. My internal thoughts continue: This photo is a representation of a ruined state, one that captures some of her numerous affairs (roller coaster rides) and subclinical but substantial manic defenses. Her affairs catalyzed her wife's threat to end their marriage over the last several months. The roller coaster also captures the sense of guilt about the wreckage and pain she caused her wife and several close family friends during the eruption when her wife learned more about the most recent affairs.

Seemingly along a kind of different frequency, I am internally thinking about the photograph as an attempt at symbolizing how the patient is trying to do something with her pain in her free time. Photography and reading about photography have become important outlets of expression for Nina and she is proud of her work, and, even more importantly, of her capacity to sometimes make use of her time in constructive, creative ways.

There are several elements of a highly challenging, refractory erotic transference that are also expressed in a new way through this action. At various times the patient has explicitly spoken of her wish to "just end the analysis and become lovers." At times she has been angry about whether in the analysis she is "being fucked with rather than fucked" and if not fucked, she is not sure about the point of being in analysis. The patient has eroticized an early maternal transference toward me in which intercourse has replaced holding and sucking. In this mode, her compulsive questions to me about whether I would want to have sex with her and find her desirable stand in for questions that she has stated explicitly about whether her parents wanted her as a child.

In her provocations, Nina is at some level asking a question now about whether she was a wanted child and whether she is someone in the analysis whom I regret taking on. And of course, it is not entirely surprising that no matter how much I care about and am invested in her, there are moments when I feel burdened, sometimes assaulted by her. Related to this sense of assault, she and I have examined how her affairs with both women and men have enacted anger and revenge toward her symbolic mother and father. We have come to understand that she reflexively rejects her wife's love and desire partly because it marks the awareness of those from whom she wanted love and by whom she was disappointed.

As she settles into the hour, Nina begins to talk about the weekend that she had spent with her wife when she photographed the roller coaster. She described feeling close to her wife and that it was easier to feel calm and less restless. Then she asks me what I think about the photograph. I take up that she may be trying to find a way to reflect on the experience of being out of control. I suggest that taking pictures and bringing in these parts of her is partly in the service of asking me to help her contain that which she has said about herself, "drives" me crazy. I tell her that the photo itself may be a way to reflect on her inner life and to make her dysregulation stand still for a moment.

I am also thinking to myself at a very speculative level about whether her dead or ruined roller coaster might constitute a protean way of grieving the fact that we will not fulfill her fantasy of going on that kind of exciting ride together. But I am internally suspicious of this kind of thinking because I know how much I want her to stop being so concrete and pressuring about wanting to have sex. So perhaps I am wishing that grieving was in the air because I would see it as a respite of sorts.

After I comment on her showing me the photograph as an attempt to capture something inside her that often will not hold still, she says, "You can't handle the part of me that acts out all of the time or that wants for us to have sex. You use your comments and interpretations as a way to not go there." This is not an uncommon response to my interpretations for her. She has often found it funny that she has developed a line of interpretation in which she frames my attempt to understand her as a defense against her notion of the analytic setting as a romantic scene. There is a greater sense of self-awareness about the absurd quality of her attempts to undermine or undo our work. She is increasingly feeling the aggressive and destructive part of her eroticism with others and with me in relation to the analytic setting.

I conjecture here that bringing in this photo marked the beginning of a transition from being quite suspicious of any sort of interpretation as "avoidance of us being together sexually," a point of view that, in her concreteness, was even humorous to her. Nina knew that in classifying interpretation and analysis itself as a resistance to entering into her versions of a setting, she was constructing/revealing a new setting of a sexual liaison. She sometimes joked that "instead of physical touch, you give me psychical touch." In this form of word and ideational play there is a "ventilated space," (Green, 1975) created when she observes her attempt to destroy the setting as an object. Unfortunately, though, she frequently reverted quite quickly into the most concrete variations of this fantasy as a reality that she was trying to institute in the analytic setting.

Over many weeks of analytic work, Nina was gradually interested in the ruined roller coaster as a symbol of her failed manic defenses.

She was already tiring of the meaninglessness of her affairs and the pain that she was causing her wife. She still frequently experienced analysis as depriving and persecutory in the absence of physical touch and overt verbal expressions of love. Yet over time she became more curious about how compulsively she had organized contact with others in relation to the fantasy of flight from painful abandonment and neglect. The awareness of the destruction that she had wrought with her wife and friends provided some motivation to engage less frequently in compulsively driven sexual liaisons. She began to feel sadder about what we were doing together, and she could better take in my attempt to hold multiple levels of reality, particularly related to her unconscious transformation of inchoate experience into something more integrated. Her compulsive joking in response to interpretation disappeared.

Nina's attempts to examine through words the meaning of her photo and her concretized version of an out of control self during this brief section of analysis marked the beginning of a transition from an autistic-contiguous mode into one in which she could tolerate her rage, longings, and sadness for slightly longer periods of time. Despite her massive doubts about the process, not long after in her analysis, she asked whether I was able to offer her a regular fifth hour. Nina claimed that it was the only thing that I could do to demonstrate my caring about her if physical contact was not in the offing. The setting became a site of some developing sense of feeling cared for. It was still a very limited setting representing the food and shelter that her parents had provided her even in the context of their emotional deprivation and harsh expectations for performance and compliance.

In expressing her gratitude, Nina introduced another form of play through a new iteration of the familiar joke—"the food is terrible, and the portions are too small." The setting was beginning to represent for her a form of feeling cared for (a larger portion of not very good food) even as her defensive minimization of the setting concealed her gratitude. The patient's depiction of the setting in her form of play could be seen as a dream, a scene that condenses her various needs: the need to express gratitude; the need for a protective enclave to partially disguise her shift into the new ideational and emotional possibility of feeling cared for; and the need for a setting to express anger at her parents and at me, and to use devaluation of the analysis to titrate her longings. In Green's terms, the framing structure can tolerate the absence of representation because it holds the psychic space, like Bion's container. Obviously, the grievance and failings of the analysis continued with the fifth hour but she had accomplished a sense of conveying her desires in a new way that was consistent with the analyst's offering of a setting, one in which she or he is both the holder/manager of the setting as well as an object of displacement and transference in the setting.

Clinical Vignette 2

In Chapter 1, I described a young man, Sam, who displayed many anti-regressive (Sandler, 1994) tendencies in analysis, unconsciously protesting mourning both the death of his father when he was an eight-year-old boy as well as feelings of loss toward his often-preoccupied mother. Here I want to try to put into focus Sam's relationship to the setting.

Sam rejected many interpretations about avoidance of his own longings, sadness, and tenderness, and while he reliably attended his four times a week analysis, he protested the very idea that we could make meaning of his experience. He demonstrated many forms of devaluing the analyst well described by Meltzer's (1975) notion of "dismantling." For this patient the setting of psychoanalytic work mirrored his experience of his mother as a manager of him and of her anxiety about loss. He could not consciously believe in the setting of analysis as anything but a repetition of maternal neglect. Seen in Blegerian terms, his actual use of the setting in his regular attendance and commitment to treatment despite his nihilism in the transference was a very good example of the non-process of the setting providing something that he could believe in—if we infer belief from his capacity to attend sessions.

Several years into the analysis, Sam invented a new setting for analysis, a fantasy in which I was to leave the office while he stayed, and we would work remotely. The fantasy of his new setting continued to express elements of negative transference and possibly a recreation of his experience of the death of his father when he was eight years old, as well as his unconscious attempt to master that loss.

It also marked a new form of play with his anxiety about growing tenderness toward both his girlfriend and me. His new analytic setting paradoxically included me in his pain by recognizing that he was not entirely asking me to leave him alone; a new form of play involving a new masquerade, hide and seek, or a game of dominance and submission was emerging. In Winnicott's statement of a particular developmental paradox: "that in order for the object to be created, it must be found," we could say that my patient was beginning to create a new analytic setting by finding parts of himself and me, but finding required titration of longing and need. Play often occurs in relationship to the setting, particularly in subverting time and other boundaries.

For this patient the setting held some of his most disturbing feelings and mine that were constantly being enacted in the analytic relationship. It is also true that the setting held my patient and me as we continually tried to construct imagery of absence and to create understandings of the collision between his internal setting and the analytic setting. Non-process and process elements were often in dynamic interplay with one another. There is an evolution over time in which the process and its elements, including the holding and containing capacities of the analyst and patient, are transferred onto the setting. The setting in this sense both represents and embodies the history, the expectation that experiences and markers of the analytic process will be constant even during and after disruptions (e.g. Lafarge 2018a.b.). These disruptions may be caused by the effects of deep interpretive work such as the transformation of beta elements into alpha elements or through attacks on the setting by patient or analyst.

Concluding Remarks

I have suggested that the setting constitutes a spatiotemporal structure, a metaphoric space in which patient and analyst try to catch hold of transitions from unrepresented to represented states. I have also suggested that we cannot make clear distinctions between the object in the setting and the setting in the object. The setting provides an auxiliary function for the analyst's capacities involving holding, containment and interpretation. The setting embodies in material and psychic form the dialectic between interpretation as a relational and a cognitive function. Finally, I have suggested that the setting is that metaphoric and material space which institutes the rules of the analytic process, rules that the patient will work with and react against. I am reminded of Wallace Stevens' (1941) characterization of poetry in connection with the setting: "a violence from within that protects us from a violence without."

Despite potential vagaries, as a metaphoric concept the setting helps us describe both interpretive and non-interpretive factors in therapeutic action. Many experienced analysts come to understand that they have therapeutic successes that do not seem to be easily explained by our models of therapeutic action. In some analyses the setting becomes almost a place of hope when interpretation and verbal-symbolic modalities are experienced as less effective than we wish. In some of our most difficult cases, the setting is the foxhole where analytic agnostics (patients and analysts) may find solace and holding that are not linked to conscious understanding. Of course, the setting may also become an object of displacement for some of the most challenging feelings that are experienced by patient and analyst.

I conjecture that our focus on the setting has also been partially sutured to our greater appreciation of the non-interpretive factors in analytic work. As psychoanalytic theory has evolved, we needed a heuristic framework, a psychic location that helped us better understand non-verbal, semiotic, implicit dimensions of clinical work as well as those involving language and knowledge.

Implicit in what I have examined regarding the object in the setting and the setting in the object is the inextricable relationship between interpretation and object relationship that is held in the setting (Aulignier, 1975) . One of the most significant shifts in psychoanalytic theory over the last 100 years is that we are generally moving away from a reductionist debate about whether interpretation or object relationship is the more exclusive or better contributor to therapeutic action in analysis. I like the way Ogden (2004a) has expressed that he takes for granted that an object relationship is a form of interpretation and that interpretation is a form of object relationship.

Finally, the setting holds a frontier of meanings that are being and not yet being communicated (Winnicott, 1963a). These states evade our understanding but allow us at moments to understand something new.

These transitional states from unrepresented to represented experience underscore the dynamic and changing nature of the setting and of psychoanalysis itself. It is this transitional state that so characterizes the nature of play and why play is the thing in analytic work.

Note

1 With much thanks to Christopher Lovett, Lucy Lafarge, Bruce Reis, Richard Zimmer, Adrienne Harris, and Kenneth Corbett. Sections of this chapter first appeared in the *International Journal of Psychoanalysis* 100.

References

Aulignier, P. (1975) *The Violence of Interpretation: From Pictogram to Statement*. London: New Library of Psychoanalysis.

Bass, A. (2007) When the frame doesn't fit the picture. *Psychoanal. Dial.* 17: 1–27.

Bion, W. R. (1959) Attacks on linking. In: *Second Thoughts* (pp. 93–109). New York: Aronson.

Bleger, J. (1967a) Psycho-analysis of the psycho-analytic frame. *Int. J. Psychoanal.* 48: 511–519.

Bleger, J. (1967b) *Symbiosis and Ambiguity: A Psychoanalytic Study*. London: New Library of Psychoanalysis.

Brenner, C. (1979) The components of psychic conflict and its consequences in mental life. *Psychoanal Q.* 48: 547–567.

Brown, L. (2015) Ruptures in the analytic setting. *Psychoanal. Q.* 84: 841–865.

Cooper, S. (2009) Familiar and unfamiliar forms of interaction in the ending phases of analysis. *Psychoanal. Dial.* 19(5): 588–603.

Cooper, S. (2010) *A Disturbance in the Field: Essays in Transference-Countertransference*. London: Routledge.

Cooper, S. (2018) Playing in the darkness: The use of the object and use of the subject. *J. Amer. Psychoanal. Assn.* 66: 173–187; Plenary address, The American Psychoanalytic Association, New York, February 16, 2018.

Feldman, M. (1997) Projective identification: The analyst's contribution. *Int. J. Psychoanal.* 78: 227–241.

Freud, S. (1914) Remembering, repeating, and working through. *S.E.* 12: 147–156.

Freud, S. (1915) Observations on transference love (Further recommendations on the technique of psychoanalysis, II). *S.E.* 12: 377–391.

Freud, S. (1920) Beyond the pleasure principle. *S.E.* 18.

Goldberg, P. (1989) Actively seeking the holding environment—conscious and unconscious elements in the building of a therapeutic framework. *Contemp. Psychoanal.* 25:448–466.

Goldberg, P. (2017) Reconfiguring the frame as a dynamic structure. In: *Reconsidering the Moveable Frame in* Psychoanalysis, Tylim, I. and Harris, A. (eds). pp. 92–111. New York: Routledge.

Goldberg, P. (2009) With respect to the analytic frame. Commentary on a paper by Steven Stern. *Psychoanal. Dialogues.* 19: 669–674.

Green, A. (1975) The analyst, symbolization, and absence in the analytic setting (on changes in analytic practice and analytic experience) – in memory of D. W. Winnicott. *Int. J. Psych-Anal.* 56: 9–22.

Green, A. (1997) The intuition of the negative in playing and reality. *Int. J. Psycho-Anal.* 78: 1071–1084.

Greenberg, J. (1995) Psychoanalytic technique and the interactive matrix. *Psychoanal. Q.* 64: 1022.

Huizinga, J. (1932) *Homo Ludens* Boston: Beacon Press.

Lafarge, L. (2018a) The imagining frame. Paper presented on Panel: Contemporary Conceptualizations of the Analytic Process, The American Psychoanalytic Association, New York.

Lafarge, L. (2018b) Termination and repetition: The dissolution of the frame. Paper presented at the IJP Centenary, Rye Brook, New York. October 2018.

Laplanche, J. (1999) *Essays on Otherness*. London: Routledge.

Lemma, A. (2014) The body of the analyst and the analytic setting: Reflections on the embodied setting and the symbiotic transference. *Int. J. Psycho-Anal.* 95: 225–244.

Meltzer, D. (1975) *Explorations in Autism*. Paris: Payot.

Modell, A. H. (1976) The holding environment and the therapeutic action of psychoanalysis. *J. Amer. Psychoanal. Assn.* 24: 258–307.

Modell, A. H. (1989) The psychoanalytic setting as a container for multiple levels of reality: A perspective on the theory of psychoanalytic treatment. *Psychoanal. Inq.* 9: 67–87.

Ogden, T. (1991) Analyzing the matrix of transference. *Int. J. Psycho-Anal.* 72: 593–605.

Ogden, T. (1994) *Subjects of Analysis*. London: Karnac.

Ogden, T. (2004a) On holding and containing, being and dreaming. *Int. J. Psycho-Anal.* 85(6): 1349–1364.

Parsons, M. (2007) Raiding the inarticulate: The internal setting and listening beyond countertransference. *Int. J. Psycho-Anal.* 88: 1441–1456.

Pontalis, J. (1997) *Ce Temps Qui Ne Passé Pas*. Paris: Gallimard.

Quinodoz, D. (1992) The psychoanalytic setting as the instrument of the container function. *Int. J. Psycho-Anal.* 73: 627–635.

Sandler, J. and Sandler, A. M. (1994) Theoretical and technical comments on regression and anti-regression. *Int. J. Psychoanal.* 75(3):431–439.

Segal, H. (1962) The curative factors in psycho-analysis: Contributions to discussion. *Int. J. Psycho-Anal.* 43: 212–213.

Steiner, J. (2006) Interpretive enactment in the analytic setting. *Int. J. Psycho-Anal.* 37: 315–320.

Stevens, W. (1941) *The Noble Rider and the Sound of Words.* Princeton: Lecture at Princeton University.

Winnicott, D. (1956) Primary maternal preoccupation. In: *The Maturational Processes and the Facilitating Environment* (pp. 300–305). New York: International University Press.

Winnicott, D. (1963a) Communicating and not communicating, leading to study of certain opposites. In: *The Maturational Processes and the Facilitating Environment* (pp. 179–192). New York: International University Press.

Winnicott, D. (1963b) The development of the capacity for concern. In: *The Maturational Process and the Facilitating Environment: Studies in the Theory of Emotional Development.* New York: Internaitonal Universities Press.

Winnicott, D. W. (1968) Playing: Its theoretical status in the clinical situation. *Int. J. Psycho-Anal.* 49:591–599.

Winnicott, D. (1969) The use of an object. *Int. J. Psycho-Anal.* 50: 711–716.

Chapter 6

"I Want You to Be": Thinking about Winnicott's View of Interpretation in Ontological and Epistemological Psychoanalysis

Winnicott's body of work may be understood as a search to find a place for living and play. As he located these places in infant development and beyond, he consistently elaborated the facilitating environment in which this growth occurs. By definition, that which is facilitative exists in a specific developmental time for the child. Being is located in time.

Ogden (2019) creatively linked the revolutionary work of Winnicott and Bion, distinct as their theories are, as part of a shift in psychoanalytic work from the epistemological to the ontological. Playing and dreaming, the central metaphoric constructs of Winnicott and Bion respectively, superseded knowing and understanding, which are featured in the theories of Freud and Klein.

The word "ontological" refers to the understanding of being. In this chapter, I will try to delve further into how being and playing were uniquely addressed by Winnicott in his understanding of interpretation. Specifically, I will explore how for Winnicott, the particular attributes of the psychoanalytic setting always contain a tension between who we are and who we are becoming. Furthermore, I will explore how sometimes the distinctions between knowing and being are less apparent than the inextricable links between the two processes. Play is an important part of how meaning and being come together.

In order to study the tension between who we are and who we are becoming, I will examine a part of Hannah Arendt's (1953) definition of love. Borrowed from Augustine, her notion is that love is expressed in the sentiment and intention: "I want you to be." I will probe how in the analytic setting, the analyst holds two different

DOI: 10.4324/9781003265078-7

attitudes in various states of integration and disequilibrium: "I want you to be" is held in concert with "I want to help you to be who you are becoming." A paradox in the analytic setting is always "in play." This paradox involves a therapeutic strategy aiming to help the patient "to be" as they are while helping the patient to experience oneself in new and different ways.

Winnicott's radical understanding of interpretation as a relational and intersubjective event rather than simply the conveyance of understanding of unconscious conflict and fantasy sets the stage for understanding the tensions between who we are and who we are becoming. Psychoanalysis has tended to focus on the meaning of "interpret" as helping to expound or explain the meaning of affect, behavior or unconscious processes. It is fair to say that in the last 70 years or so the part of the word "inter" has occupied a great deal of our attention. "Inter" means between and focuses more on a translation of meaning between two people. Much of Winnicott's work focused on the particular ways that an object can meet the patient to promote growth in various developmental stages. I consider how for Winnicott, the analyst's intention or desire to help the patient to be and to become is a unique and thus different way of thinking about ontological analysis than Bion's ideal of being without memory and desire.

Winnicott understood interpretation as functioning to convey to the patient the limits of his understanding. A central tenet of his theory was expressing an analytic attitude that went beyond his modesty, an attitude examining how play can be discovered between something old and something new. He was putting forward the notion of interpretation as a metaphoric squiggle game, one in which the notion of limitation is the place from which productive, collaborative meaning and being are built. It is, in a sense, "the place where we live" (Winnicott, 1971).

Incorporating the notion that all of psychoanalysis involves enactment, interpretation enacts a wish to offer and the limitation in doing so. It is in this seam of offering and limitation that the analyst is also becoming something new with his patient. Winnicott's notion of "giving back" is the lynchpin of interpretation. Giving back preserves the possibility that the patient may continue to work, serving to develop and reaffirm the setting of psychoanalysis. The reinforcement of the setting provides a place for the individual to live and become in time. It is in the analytic setting that for Winnicott, meaning and being are fused.

Winnicott's Contribution to the Understanding of Interpretation

Winnicott's revolutionary contributions to the understanding of what constitutes an interpretation are the outcome of a few dozen papers about how environment facilitates the infant becoming a person. Winnicott introduced an intersubjective level of participation in interpretation: he emphasized the necessity of the analyst's psychological work with his own depression and his own relationship with his mother in allowing for interpretation to have traction with some patients; he spoke of interpretation as a kind of holding *in time* akin to the mother's holding the infant in time; he highlighted the importance of the patient's acclimation to the analyst along with the analyst finding the patient's place of maximal receptivity; and he emphasized how interpretation functions in part to show the patient the analyst's limitations in knowing the patient at any moment *in time*.

Winnicott's paper on interpretation (1968a), vastly underemphasized in its importance, is an indispensable companion to his well-known paper, "The Use of the Object: Relating through identifications" (Winnicott, 1969). In his paper on interpretation, he also described how an analyst can make himself useful to his patient. In order to do so, the analyst uses interpretation to continually support the potential space provided in the analytic setting. And as background to his paper on interpretation, his essay "The Place Where We Live" (Winnicott, 1968) along with his paper on transitional objects (Winnicott, 1971) laid the foundation for ontological analysis. For Winnicott, interpretation marks the boundary of the analyst's understanding while buttressing the potential space that can augment that understanding. In other words, patient and analyst live another day through the analytic setting for the future possibility that they will augment that understanding.

Winnicott raises the following question in "The Place Where We Live": "Here are two places then, the inside and outside of the individual, but is this all?" (Winnicott, 1968, p. 222). Winnicott was highly unsatisfied with the observation that most psychoanalytic writing influenced by Freud and Klein dwelled either on the individual's relationship to objects or else on the inner life of the individual. While he is profoundly interested in what we are doing (e.g. playing and using, which comprise a great deal of the final phase of his psychoanalytic writing), in this essay he raises the question of where we are when we are doing, "if we are anywhere at all" (p. 222).

While he doesn't say it explicitly in this paper, this is of course a place where we live in psychoanalysis as patient and analyst. For Winnicott, psychoanalysis is partly doing because it involves playing. Winnicott felt that psychoanalysis had never addressed the matter of how the experiences of the individual person (baby, child, adult) interacting with the environment result in playing and cultural experience. He felt the need for a third concept beyond the concept of inner and outer, suggesting *potential space* as the place for creative playing and for cultural experience to occur. Potential space is the hypothetical area between the baby and the object mother during the phase of the repudiation of the object as not-me. Potential space is created as merger with the mother is concluded.

Winnicott is continually interested in where and how play occurs. He emphasized that we need a place for the experience of subjectivity from the beginning of development. In "Primitive Emotional Development," Winnicott sketches a location where the infant develops trust that there is a subjective presence before they can experience subjectivity. In the transitional object paper, he delineates a space for the first not-me possession, a space to hold illusion. In "The Place Where We Live," playing and cultural experience take up space and time and help to link the past, present, and future. This third space is neither inside the individual nor strictly outside in the realm of shared reality. Within potential space is the negation of separation and space between infant and mother. It is the foundation of the baby's trust in the mother experienced over long intervals at the very beginning of separation of not-me from me. It marks the beginning of an autonomous self. Winnicott has now completed a great deal of the work involved in location and time problems that served as theoretical backdrops for his papers "Interpretation in Psychoanalysis" (Winnicott, 1968) and "The Use of the Object" (Winnicott, 1969).

In his paper on interpretation (Winnicott, 1968), arresting in the simplicity with which he explicates extremely complex ideas, Winnicott (1968) emphasizes how frequently interpretations in psychoanalysis do not reach the patient. Like Balint (1968), he was concerned with the potential for interpretation to indoctrinate the patient.

Winnicott (1968, p. 254) suggests that the best types of interpretations "give back to the patient what the patient has communicated." By giving back the interpretation to the patient, the patient is enabled to correct misunderstandings. Importantly, Winnicott emphasizes that interpretation, the giving back to the patient of what he or she has said, occurs *in real time*. The patient is communicating within the reality of transference with all of the selective perception that is implied by transference, and the analyst offers what he or she has heard in that moment. The patient receives what can be received within their varieties of dissociated states, defenses, or limited transference in a moment of time. Winnicott focuses on the ways that what the analyst says must be fresh.

This way of locating the patient's receptivity to interpretation is the correlate of all of Winnicott's work to precisely locate the patient's capacities for object relating in time and space. In primitive emotional development, he was defining a particular matrix in which the infant and mother can begin to be separately located in time and space. In the transitional object phase, what permits the infant to develop further capacities to appraise another person is the precision of the first me/not-me possession, one in which the mother holds the me/not-me paradox, honoring the importance of illusion. Giving back in the transitional object stage of relating might involve simply (not so simply, actually) honoring the patient's illusions about who or what is under the control of the patient and what is not.

For Winnicott, eventually the mother must survive destruction in order to make use of the object. So perhaps we could say that Winnicott is writing a paper here on interpretation that could read as "The Capacity to Receive an Interpretation" and "The Capacity to Make an Interpretation".

By giving back, potential space in the analytic situation is held by the analyst; in a sense, the setting of analysis is preserved by the giving back of interpretation. There is a place for the patient to become who he is; to find meaning and play with the feelings and words he has expressed and that the analyst has expressed. There is a place to live, play and make use of the patient's being and becoming. Epistemology and ontology are, for Winnicott, not sharp divides.

Here is a common, brief example of giving back. A female patient in her early 20s was realizing the pain that she had wrought on her parents through some of her recent behavior. She felt that she had flaunted her anger at them and said things to them that she regretted. She said with a voice of incredulity, "What comes to mind is that I was foolish. Like I see something about this, about how much my anger toward them about so many things came out all at once. They would have no idea how to take it in. Now that I see it, it seems ..." and she paused for what seemed like a long time. I said, "Shocking?" She said, "Well, not really shocking. I'm more like awestruck." I said, "Because you're taking it in. You're not shocked because you're realizing something about it." She said, "Yes, I'm feeling myself with them and what I did; that it really hurts to feel something about the way that I hurt them. And it's foolish. I never use that word." I said, "Maybe foolish because you recognize that there was a hope of feeling understood. You created them as capable of understanding even as you were so angry." She sighed and seemed sad as she agreed.

Giving back involves the metaphoric, verbal usage of the squiggle game with adults. The analyst holds potential space in the analytic situation so that the patient can be held in a back and forth. A large function of holding the setting is to hold the patient in time, which is emphasized by how the limits of interpretation are the beginning of the next iteration of expressiveness. The limits of interpretation mark how potential space is where becoming (i.e. trying to arrive at a sense of things) finds a home. Interpreting the content of unconscious fantasy and transference is not of primary importance, though that doesn't mean that play doesn't have meaning. Play does have meaning and meaning-making is part of what contributes to being. Play is an important part of how meaning and being come together.

In this example, I felt an impulse to bring the patient into a headier but perhaps important possibility: "Did you perhaps want to hurt or retaliate against your parents? Are you furious and are there reasons that you expressed things this way that we will hopefully look into?" I believe that this is the type of remark that Winnicott wrote about regretting throughout his career because he found these moments to be better served by holding back this comment and waiting for the patient to arrive at this awareness. The analyst is required to trust that there will be a "time" and a "place" for being able to investigate these matters, most likely initiated by the patient. I am often unable to hold back from this type of elaboration and I would say that there are times when it appears useful and times when I have just exercised my formulation skills.

In the ensuing weeks, this patient found herself in a similar moment of expressed anger and regret toward her parents. She eventually arrived at a very sad and important moment of awareness when she said: "I think that I'm punishing them less because of what they did but more because they don't seem capable of understanding that I'm angry about it." This realization echoed the comment that I had made about why she felt foolish, but it was a deeper point of arrival when she experienced it more directly.

An even more subtle section of the interpretation paper is the humanistic and ontological view of what an interpretation is and how it functions in analysis. Winnicott's "Interpretation in Psychoanalysis" is essentially his view of how the patient makes use of the analyst and how the analyst can make himself available for usage. He discusses how patients learn the interpretive style of their analysts, likening the way that patients get used to their analyst's styles of interpreting to how children learn to take in the best of their parents and acclimate to their parents' limitations in parenting. Winnicott here is echoing some of his earliest, pioneering observations from his 1945 paper, "Primitive Emotional Development" in which he underscores the patient's experience of the analyst's internal objects and whether or not the analyst has worked out their own depressive experiences.

With Winnicott's (1971) paper on interpretation, interpretation has moved far outside the epistemological realm related to the content of unconscious conflict, defense, unconscious fantasy, and internalized object relation. In this single paper, a summary of his work in many ways, Winnicott has described a shift from epistemological approaches to interpretation to the notion that interpretations involve an experience between patient and analyst. Winnicott is essentially asserting that all interpretations are a form of object relation and all object relations carry elements of interpretive understanding, a point that Ogden (2004) has usefully elaborated.

As I explore later in the chapter, Winnicott is also interested in how the analyst can have hopes for who the patient might become without influencing the patient's own aims for becoming. For Winnicott, interpretation is a form of therapeutic activity and while it is a vehicle for therapeutic action in terms of what it communicates, the activity is a thing unto itself. Playing is the thing. He has shifted Klein's emphasis on the content of play and its meaning regarding unconscious fantasy toward finding new and future capacities for playing.

What Do We Mean by Being and Being in Time?

Hannah Arendt (1958, p. 57, 1996), borrowing Augustine's phrase, "Volu ut sis" (I want you to be) defined love in the following way:

This mere existence, that is, all that which is mysteriously given to us by birth and which includes the shape of our bodies and the talents of our minds, can be adequately dealt with only by the unpredictable hazards of friendship and sympathy, or by the great and incalculable grace of love, which says with Augustine, "Volo ut sis" (I want you to be), *without being able to give any particular reason for such supreme and unsurpassable affirmation.*

The "I want" part of this statement involves something finite, limited, and may include demand. "I want you to be" steps back from ownership and possession (*Cupiditas*), recognizing the individual as he is (*Caritas*), *now*. The recognition of someone as they are now is what I mean by "in time."

It seems to me that psychoanalysis lives paradoxically in the seam between the two parts of this definition of love. The analyst who is working ontologically wants to help his patient to be and to become who they are. Yet the analyst's wanting for the patient in this regard will sometimes create a disruption in the patient's current state of being. Even an analyst who has relatively easy access to acceptance of the patient may be perceived by the patient as too disruptive or even destructive. Other patients may experience it as exciting or over-stimulating. Ontological psychoanalysis as Ogden (2019) has distilled it in the theories of Winnicott and Bion is no less influenced by this complexity than epistemological approaches to psychoanalysis.

Using different theoretical models, Winnicott (1945) and Loewald (1960) share a developmental perspective about growth in the analytic situation that is relevant to the "I want" part of what the analyst feels. They each highlight a tension between acceptance of the patient and a sense of futurity about the patient's growth. In a sense, they each authorized the psychic future (Cooper, 1997), giving it more power in relation to the "authority of the past" (Chodorow, 1996, p. 65). However, they differ on the epistemological axis in ways that are important in understanding tensions between being and becoming.

Loewald (1960) viewed interpretation as taking a patient one step into regression and one step into a kind of psychic future. Loewald was keenly interested in the question of how the analyst relates to and represents aspects of the patient's growth and future resulting from the analytic process. Loewald took this discussion for the first time out of the realm of pathological countertransference and more into the routine aspects of how analysis works. Loewald was also beginning to address the analyst's symbolic function in therapeutic action, i.e. that the analyst and the analytic process itself can represent growth and aspects of the patient's psychic future. However, he did not explore the experience of the analyst and the variety of ways of thinking about the analyst's wishes for the patient to change. Instead, Loewald's view of the analyst was implicitly based in an epistemological position in which the analyst should be objective and stand for the possibility of a more objective appraisal of psychic reality.

Here is a typical example of what Loewald had in mind regarding the regressive and progressive elements of interpretation. An analyst comes to see that his patient smiles whenever he feels threatened. The analyst might be aware that his patient is trying to put a happy face on something painful. Simultaneously, the analyst might try to help the patient feel a possibility that he might bear his pain without needing to cover it up. The analyst wants the patient "to be" whether he needs to hide his pain or not, but he imagines for the patient a psychic possibility in which it does not need to be covered up. Taking it even further, perhaps sometimes the analyst, by wanting his patient to be, is imagining that the patient can be sad without having to cover it up. So, in this sense, wanting the patient to be is consistent with the analyst's wishes or intentions for the patient to be able to grow.

Returning to my earlier brief vignette, I might want to accept my patient's recognition that her anger was something that her parents couldn't understand. At the same time, however, I might have harbored a strong desire to help her realize that she had an unconscious retaliatory wish. In helping her to recognize this retaliatory motive, I might imagine that it would be easier for her to release her anger. The analyst is potentially pulled in at least two incompatible directions in wanting his patient to be. For example, I want my patient to feel her feelings of guilt or regret for punishing her parents, but I might also want her to understand why she might wish to punish them. These two feelings are not yet something that she can integrate, and I cannot know whether she will ever be able to do so.

Winnicott differs from Loewald along the epistemological axis in that the analyst is viewed as in a process of finding, participating in, and supervising play. For Winnicott, the analyst is a co-participant in play, not entirely inhabiting the same role as the patient but with intrinsic overlap during the process of play. Rather than postulating more maturity and objectivity, he is conceptualized as failing through interpretation, which is paradoxically an offering for the patient to build on what they are learning.

Winnicott's offering resides in what is provided and the limitations in what is provided. Winnicott (1945; 1949) did believe that the analyst must be analyzed and trained as well as possible in order to work out his own internalized relationship to maternal objects, particularly his relationship to maternal depression, in order to be as facilitative as possible. In contrast to Loewald, though, play introduced implicit elements of symmetry between patient and analyst that are always in dialectical tension with the asymmetry of the analytic relationship.

For Winnicott, it seems reasonable to assume that a tension between acceptance of the patient as they are and a sense of their potential futurity is contained in the notion that being and the process of becoming are one. I believe that Winnicott quite uniquely held this "oneness" in his analytic attitude toward play and interpretation. If we consider these matters with regard to time, it could be said that the analyst is trying to appreciate the patient's current adaptation in any particular moment. It is not an accident that Winnicott leaned into the term "capacity," emphasizing the patient's capacity to integrate "bit and pieces" of who they are at any given moment. Regarding the psychic future, though, "I want you to be" might be translated as "I also want you to be in a way that you have not yet felt that you could be."

Returning to the concept of "giving back" (Winnicott, 1968), we can see this complexity in full force since it requires a particular kind of developmental/analytic setting in order to "give back." Is the notion of Winnicott's various forms of a facilitating environment and object responsiveness consistent with Bion's axiom, a paraphrase from T. S. Eliot's (1963) "Four Quartets," for the analyst to be without memory and desire? In using this phrase, Bion was addressing his monumental project of how to find a listening position in which we are not carrying forward meanings that obscure the understanding of emergent unconscious meaning. Winnicott was interested in this project as well. We could say that Bion's notion of dreaming the patient involves an anticipation of becoming. But Winnicott seems to have had some concern with Bion's use of Eliot's phrase. In a letter to Bion in October of 1967 (Winnicott, 1968), after hearing the lecture in which Bion made the statement, Winnicott wrote of his objections. Eliot had used this phrase to refer to a quality of leaves buried in snow during winter. Winnicott is disturbed by Bion's stated ideal to listen without memory and desire since for Winnicott, the word "desire" resides more exclusively in the subjective realm and is thus more suited to the poetry from which the phrase is derived than to psychoanalysis. He proposes for himself a preferred word, "intention," one that he feels is more respectful of the reality of the patient's separateness as outside his own omnipotent control. Winnicott is quick to point out, however, that Bion himself suggested that we each have to find our own words for describing the need to be watchful of our imposition of psychic reality on to our patients.

I draw the reader's attention to this letter because the complexity of Winnicott's term "holding"—for the individual "to be known in all his bits and pieces" in time (Winnicott, 1945, p. 150)—and Loewald's (1960) notion of anticipating the patient's psychic future are overlapping, and perhaps different than Bion's clinical ideal of being without memory and desire. Winnicott is enthusiastic about the analyst using interpretation to enhance the patient's ability to grow, if only we don't get in the way too much. Both Bion and Winnicott are profoundly concerned with the analyst imposing meaning, but Winnicott's writing is filled with the value of being met by a particular kind of object. This externality in some ways poses problems for the patient even as it promotes the patient's process of becoming. Being met implies futurity and future growth. I believe that it involves memory and a sense of futurity.

In my reading then, Winnicott does want and value the patient's becoming, though he *intends* as an analyst to not impose too much of that desire on to the patient. However, the analyst's "I want" may have some collision points with the patient's being. Both (Ogden, 2016) and I (Cooper, 2018) have suggested that the patient's experience of the analyst being destroyed or the threat of being destroyed is a part of what promotes a transition from object relating to object usage. This collision point is instructive because in this formulation, the analyst desires to survive the patient's destruction and at some point the patient can experience this survival. In this reading of how patients move from relating to usage, the analyst has memory and desire of feeling potentially destroyed. The analyst most definitely desires to survive. Does the patient attempt to destroy the object or destroy the analyst's desire to survive destruction?

Thus, as we have probed the concept of "giving back," we see another dimension of the concept, namely that it has a quiet intentionality. Part of the intentionality for Winnicott is to fulfill the mandate of facilitating the finding of play. Play is partly found in relation to how patients and analysts are searching for new forms of symbolized and unsymbolized experience (Cooper, 2018; Parsons, 2000; Winnicott, 1968a). Winnicott (1968a) stresses that this often requires a great deal of waiting. King (1978) captured this well in referring to another T. S. Eliot idea about how, hope, and the love are embedded in and intrinsic to waiting.

Patients and analysts are also searching for new forms of play in relation to the limits of both patient and analyst (Green, 1975; Wilson 2016, 2013). This is a different intention than earlier views of interpretation that focus more strictly on metabolization of the patient's associations, such as offered by both Strachey J. (1934) and Bion (1967). In addition to whatever metabolization may occur, Winnicott gives back to show the patient the limits of his understanding and, mostly, to preserve the setting which allows the patient to become who they are becoming. Giving back involves holding the setting and trusting the patient's capacities to listen in a way that is similar to W. Whitman's (Leaves of Grass) description of inner life. Whitman suggests through repeated metaphors that all music, the music of inner life is what awakens within us when we are reminded by our thoughts, the instruments as it were.

A few quite commonplace examples come to mind about what Winnicott might mean by "giving back" in view of futurity. A 30-year-old male patient is quite attached to his parents in a way that he feels requires him to take care of their anxiety and insecurity. His parents tend to live in an insulated way, unadventurous in their professional and interpersonal risks. The patient says one day as he lies down on the couch, "I am a mean person," after telling a story of being ignored on a visit with his family. He had felt obviously angry at his parents and this led him to say that he was mean. I said, "You are angry, but does that make you mean?" I had previously brought up his ways of protecting his family by turning against himself a few times, but in this instance, there is simply a giving back and a declaration of the undergirding of potential space. There is an implicit recognition by the analyst that to explain the motivation for turning his anger against himself in order to protect his parents is to beat a dead horse. The comment preserves the opportunity to reflect together to see what else comes up. For this patient, what immediately followed was this: "I am mean because I haven't told you some things about just wanting them to die." This was quickly undone but the unfit news to print was already out on the street. Naturally, I cannot know whether my earlier attempts to understand how he protected his family contributed to his new experience, or whether resisting an explanation of why he did this contributed to this shift.

Another patient, a male teacher, described having tears when he saw a video of his students taken over the course of the year. The video was shown at a parent event. He said, "I had such an abnormal reaction to the video. I don't have a normal reaction to something like it. I was crying and I'm pretty sure that no one else was crying." I said to him simply, "You had your reaction." The patient began sobbing, I think because it was simply this experience of having room to cry or emote in general that he had not felt in his family. This is a different way of speaking than to say, "You find a way to police your reaction rather than having it. Inside, you feel that you aren't supposed to have your own reaction." To be sure, I had said this kind of thing to this patient in the past. This raises a question again, namely about whether some kinds of epistemologically based interpretations later create a context for more ontologically based comments. Sometimes there is a presumption of simple familiarity in responsiveness that is embedded in many years of understanding parts of the patient.

I think that a more explanatory, epistemological responsiveness is sometimes the forerunner to the kind of direct, intimate, and perhaps even presumptuous language of what I said to my patient or what Ogden (2019) described with his patients. The two modes of responsiveness often work in complementary ways.

I want to underscore that often a very important part of "giving back" to the patient relates to a significant shift that has occurred in the analyst. I don't think that Winnicott made this part explicit, but it was implied in a number of his papers as he articulated his wish that he had done less explaining and more listening and giving back (e.g. Winnicott, 1969).

Perhaps these moments that I have just described at times involve the analyst resisting forcing particular ways of understanding on the patient. In this sense, "I want you to be" may be understood as an ideal held by the analyst regarding his listening position. It is also a meaningful link to Bion's ideal of trying to be without memory and desire. There is sometimes a conflict within the analyst about this intention, another meaning to Parson's (2007) observation that psychoanalysis is a contentious process. With regard to analysis being a contentious process, we could say that the analyst might feel something along these lines: "I want to want you to be, but I know that sometimes you struggle with being and I struggle being with you."

Further Understanding What We Mean by Ontological Psychoanalysis: Bridging the Epistemological and Ontological Divide

Winnicott, as a pioneer if not originator of the ontological approach, maintained that his central focus on the purpose of interpretation is showing his patients the limits of his understanding. He was not proposing modesty for modesty's sake but trying to get the analyst focused on the work at hand: namely, that facilitating growth both in development and analysis involves the parent/analyst's search for how (when possible) to be of use to the patient; this search is the other side of the patient's search for how to make use of the analyst.

What struck me in all of the excellent clinical examples of what Ogden (2019) meant by ontological analysis was a quality of an analyst ardently in search of making contact with his patient. In each of his clinical examples, it seemed to me that there was an often implicit and sometimes explicit suggestion that many early attempts at finding the patient had failed. Winnicott (1968, 1969) emphasized interpretation as an intersubjective process which included the patient's accommodation to the analyst and his interpretive style. *I take from this view of interpretation a suggestion that interpretation is both an offering and a request of the patient to find a way to make use of it (or not).*

I believe that another dimension to the ontological turn, which Winnicott, Bion, and Ogden describe, involves the analyst as "after the fall," as it were. They are presenting the analyst as someone who never should have been thought of as "knowing" to begin with. Bion's focus on unlearning overvalued ideas links him to the ways that Winnicott underscored interpretation as intrinsically limited.

In some ways, then, when Winnicott (1969) states toward the beginning of "The Use of the Object" that he has changed and how he has changed, I believe that he is describing how ontological analysis grew out of his practice of epistemological analysis. He is describing that for his patients who could not experience him as an object offering understanding, many of his observations were without meaning.

"Although it comes out of my psycho-analytical experience I would not say that it could have come out of my psycho-analytical experience of two decades ago, because I would not then have had the technique to make possible the transference movements that I wish to describe. For instance, it is only in recent years that I have become able to wait and wait for the natural evolution of the transference arising out of the patient's growing trust in the psycho-analytical technique and setting, and to avoid breaking up this natural process by making interpretations. It will be noticed that I am talking about the making of interpretations and not about interpretations as such. It appalls me to think how much deep change I have prevented or delayed in patients in a certain classification category by my personal need to interpret. If only we can wait, the patient arrives at understanding creatively and with immense joy, and I now enjoy this joy more than I used to enjoy the sense of having been clever. I think I interpret mainly to let the patient know the limits of my understanding ... " (p. 712).

I wonder whether there are ways that analysts commonly go through a process akin to this with many patients who are unable to make use of more traditional interpretations. It is true that Freudian and Kleinian approaches to interpretation are embedded in an epistemological approach and that this is quite different from ontological approaches. However, in some way, a more ontological focus follows an epistemological one even in primarily epistemological approaches. In my work, I often gradually feel more comfort and familiarity to explain less and reside more in emotional spaces with the patient. To "be" with another patient and to give back as Winnicott is describing is an extraordinarily intimate and familiar way of interacting with another person. In some ways, the understandings offered through an epistemological approach are more formal. Perhaps too, more explanatory responsiveness respects the newness of the relationship, the separateness of the analyst from the patient, and the gradualness with which one proceeds in working in analysis.

While there is no single element that characterizes an ontological analytic approach, there are a few dimensions of interpretation or perhaps more accurately, responsiveness, that stand out. These include a less formal and less explanatory way of responding. The responsiveness is direct, respectful, but also quite familiar in the sense that the analyst is saying, as it were, "I know you." It seems important that the responsiveness often arrives after the failure or limitations of previous forms of interpretation and responsiveness. Perhaps it could be said that the analyst conveys something along these lines: "I have faith in your ability to grow even if I don't always know how to facilitate that. I do believe that something about this setting and trying can be of use to the process of becoming who you are." I believe that this truly characterized Winnicott's approach to psychoanalysis and interpretation.

One factor characterizing his responsiveness is that the analyst is relaxing some of the position as interpreter. In many of the examples that I have presented in this book, I have tried to capture the evolution of my ways of helping patients to be and my ways of being with the patient. It seems to me that in many of the examples here, the analyst is to some extent relaxing some of his previous stance as interpreter. The analyst has a familiarity, a voice that is perhaps less distancing than a voice that we usually associate with interpretation.

There is intimacy that is reflected in a certain level of genuine and affectionate presumption. I think that the intimacy is partly in response to a belief in the patient's ability to grow or an acknowledgment of the growth that has already occurred.

Let's examine my example of Henry from Chapter 2 at the moment in which I asked Henry how long he "would court his anger." There is something benignly reflective, on the border between an observation and a suggestion, which is what makes it presumptuous in a familiar way. There is an almost avuncular quality to it because it issues from a place where the same suggestion by a parent might more likely be seen as intrusive or controlling. My association is to an afternoon when I was 12 on a school break and I was anxious about something. My mother noticed my anxiety and said, "Why don't you go play basketball with your friends." It had a quality of someone seeing me and loving me enough to guess what might be useful. I trusted the suggestion. She anticipated a psychic future (of my becoming more relaxed). Henry was able to trust me more deeply at the moment that I am summarizing. He noted the familiarity and intimacy with which I spoke.

In this example and most of those presented by Ogden (2019) I am speaking more *in the moment* and from *almost* outside the analytic framework. I mean, by "almost," that there is a sense of an illusion that speech is issuing from outside the analytic frame since of course everything that patient and analyst say to one another occurs inside the frame. When I asked Henry how long he would court his anger, consider how many different things might have been going on there from our highly exercised skills in analytic formulation. First it can be said that from an epistemological point of view, there may be a rather traditional formulation that might go something like this: "You have changed and gone beyond what you resented your father for. A part of you wants to hold on to this anger to punish him or claim vindication – that you had the right to your angry feelings. Yet holding on to your anger is costing you the acknowledgement of your own actual growth." Or, "You are angry at him, but you want to stay attached to him through your anger and you may not yet know how to let it go and still be attached to him." We could even speculate that the patient holds on to anger because of unresolved anger or loving feelings toward the analyst.

There are many similar formulations about why the patient might be holding on to his anger. It is possible that issuing interpretations to this effect might at some point be of use to the patient, or even already have been so, such as in the case of Henry. In fact, it might be that some of those ways of understanding the patient's holding on to anger catalyzed both the patient's and analyst's abilities to work in this moment without such formulations.

This example and some of Ogden's (2019) examples illustrate how interpretation is once again occurring in real time, concurrently based on what the analyst has to offer and his or her limitations in understanding.

In Chapter 2, I wrote about the analyst's limits regarding the patient's relationship to the bad object and how play is sometimes found in the release of the bad object. I was trying to demonstrate that the patient's and the analyst's experiences of limit are "in play" during the process of the patient's release of the bad object. The patient's and analyst's relation to the patient's internal objects, including bad and unsatisfying objects, is often where play itself begins. While a great deal of psychoanalysis has focused on Winnicott's (1951) formulation of the holding elements of transitional space and play, I have emphasized that the concept of limit is also constitutive of play. Here, "I want" by the analyst could be translated as, "I want you to stop doing this so you can be in other ways."

Let's return for a moment to Arendt's notion of love as "I want you to be" and the complexity of that sentiment in the analytic relationship. The analyst's interpretations are intended in many ways to help the patient be himself, but the patient has come to an analyst for precisely the reason that they don't know how to do that. So, interpretation is in some ways alerting the patient and analyst to the idea of wanting you to be "different" than you are, but not too different, and in so doing, becoming more yourself. We do love the patient as they are because we have come to know that they have come by their adaptation honestly. Saying to Henry in Chapter 2, "How long will you court this anger?" could be translated as: "I think that I see who you have become in a way that you may not have fully seen yet. You don't need to hold on to that anger, do you?" The formalized, ritualistic, institutionalized asymmetry of the setting has given way to shared, symmetrical elements of being human beings holding an interest. Time is in the present tense here.

Coda

The simplicity of the way that Winnicott described his concepts of giving back and interpretation belie a unique, complex amalgam of understanding and being in his version of ontological psychoanalysis. Despite the fact that Winnicott does not primarily use play to interpret unconscious meaning (e.g. Winnicott, 1971), only meaningful play can be used by the patient. It is in the finding of play that meaning and being are fused.

My reading of Winnicott is that he was not only one of the progenitors of ontological psychoanalysis, but that he also unwittingly described a process that occurs in many analyses related to a shift from an epistemological to an ontological focus. This process was also recapitulated during his career as an analyst, a movement from less explanation to more emotional responsiveness. Along these lines, we frequently observe analysts of different persuasions describing the termination stages of treatment. Their descriptions sound as though patient and analyst have found a more relaxed and different way of "being" with each other. There is less knowing and more being together, both with what has happened and what is occurring now in the context of ending. At these times, knowing is not in the foreground but is likely the undergirding for being. So, perhaps even epistemologically influenced approaches "trend" toward the ontological over time.

Thus, in addition to the quite substantial differences between epistemological and ontological approaches to psychoanalysis, I have suggested that it is often useful to think about the same piece of analytic work with each patient as having epistemological aspects and ontological aspects. Case examples from this book in Chapters 2, 3, and 4 nearly all display an evolution of responsiveness that moves from the epistemological to the ontological.

Put briefly, the analyst's attempts to know and understand his patient are sometimes the precondition for helping the patient to be and helping the analyst to find out how to be with the patient. Sometimes the opposite is true—the analyst's responsiveness to the patient's affects without explanation creates a receptivity and a thirst for explanations of what is determinative about particular experiences.

In psychoanalysis, the statement "I want you to be" implies the obvious internal struggle that we each have as persons situated in the circumstances we were in "then" and those we are in now. No matter how much our patients want to be, they also can't help but cling to painful attachments and adaptations. Analysts, no matter how much they want or intend for their patient to be and become, struggle with their own forms of resistance to facilitating this process. Analysts try to develop a capacity to titrate and monitor how strong the "I want" part in "I want you to be" is, so that it steers clear of "I need" you to be. In clinical work, as in parenting, however, the distinctions between the ways that parent/analyst can want and need are often permeable and changing.

One point of complexity about making sharp distinctions between epistemological analysis and ontological analysis is that sometimes, even our most intellectualized and formulaic interventions may contribute to a patient's growth. It is humbling that in many ways we cannot know what has been most important to the patient's growth. I believe, though, that our capacity to understand influences our ability to help our patients to be and to be with them. Our capacity to be with them helps them and us to come to know who they are.

References

Arendt, H. (1958) *The Human Condition*. Chicago: The University of Chicago Press.

Arendt, H. (1996) *Love and Saint Augustine*, ed. Joanna Vecchiarelli Scott and Judith Chelius Stark. Chicago: The University of Chicago Press.

Balint, M. (1968) *The Basic Fault*. London:Tavistock Press.

Bion, W. (1967) Notes on memory and desire. *The Psychoanalytic Forum* 2: 271–286.

Chodorow, N. (1996) Reflections on the authority of the past in psychoanalytic thinking. *Psychoanal. Q.* 65: 32–51.

Cooper, S. H. (1997) Psychoanalysis and the psychic future. *Int. J. Psycho-Anal.* 78: 667–681.

Cooper, S. H. (2018) Playing in the darkness: Use of the object and use of the subject. *J. Amer. Psychoanal. Assn.* 66(4): 743–765.

Eliot, T. S. (1963) *Collected Poems: 1909–1962*. New York, London: Harcourt, Brace & Company.

Green, A. (1975) The analyst, symbolization, and absence in the analytic setting (on changes in analytic practice and analytic experience). *Int J. Psych-Anal.* 56: 9–22.

King, P. (1978) Affective response of the analyst to the patient's to the patient's responses. *Int. J. Psycho-Anal.* 59: 329–334.

Loewald, H. (1960) On the therapeutic action of psycho-analysis. *Int. J. Psycho-Anal.* 41: 16–33.

Ogden, T. H. (2004) On holding and containing, being and dreaming. *Int. J. Psychoanal.* 85(6): 1349–1364.

Ogden, T. H. (2019) Ontological psychoanalysis or "What do you want to be when you grow up?" *Psycho. Q.* 88: 661–684.

Parsons, M. (2000) *The Dove That Returns, the Dove That Vanishes: Paradox and Creativity in Psychoanalysis*. London: Routledge.

Winnicott, D. W. (1945) Primitive emotional development. In: *Through Paediatrics in Psychoanalysis* (pp. 145–156). New York: Basic Books.

Winnicott, D. W. (1949) Hate in the countertransference. In: *Through Paediatrics in Psychoanalysis* (pp. 194–203). New York: Basic Books.

Winnicott, D. W. (1968a) Interpretation in psychoanalysis. Originally published in C. Winnicott, R. Shepherd, & M. Davis (Eds.) (1989) *Psychoanalytic Explorations* (pp. 207–212). Cambridge, MA: Harvard University Press.

Winnicott, D. W. (1968b) Playing: Its theoretical status in the clinical situation. *Int. J. Psycho-Anal.* 49: 591–599.

Winnicott, D. W. (1969) The use of an object. *Int. J. Psycho-Anal.* 50: 711–716.

Winnicott, D. W. (1971) The place where we live. In: *Playing and Reality* (pp. 104–110). London: Tavistock.

Chapter 7

Donald Winnicott's Play and Stephen Mitchell's Developmental Tilt Hypothesis Reconsidered [1]

Introduction

Stephen Mitchell was a brilliant theoretician and an equally brilliant rhetorician. Mitchell's (1984) trenchant critique of object relations theory, including the works of Klein, Fairbairn, Balint, Winnicott, Guntrip, Kernberg, Modell, and Kohut, provided a heuristic lens to better understand some of the blind spots in the theoretical advances of object relations theory.

It was Mitchell's hypothesis that these different types of object relations theory had in common an attempt to preserve elements of drive theory by attributing the development of object relations to a pre-Oedipal period of development. Mitchell wanted to draw attention to the potential misuses of the "developmental tilt," in which particular kinds of life cycle relational issues are collapsed into their earliest manifestations. His thesis was that these theoreticians used this collapse to understand later developmental epochs through the lens of drive-related issues. I am mostly in agreement with his thesis regarding Fairbairn, Guntrip, Kohut, and American Ego Psychology, each of whom contributed in unique ways to the understanding of object relations.

However, I contend and interrogate that the revolutionary contributions of Donald Winnicott were not well understood within Mitchell's (1984) developmental tilt hypothesis. I will explore some ways that Mitchell overlooked how Winnicott radicalized what it is to live a psychic life, to be in psychoanalysis as a patient and analyst, and why it matters. It's unfortunate that the independent and

DOI: 10.4324/9781003265078-8

relational traditions have not had a more active and fruitful conversation. That conversation has been taking place, de facto, through the work of analysts who have taken up Winnicott's concepts while elaborating elements of the analyst's subjectivity (e.g. Benjamin, 1990, 2004; Bromberg, 1996; Cooper, 2000, 2018, 2019, 2021, 2022; Fabozzi, 2016; Grossmark, 2016; Ogden, 2016; Pizer, 1996; Roussillon, 2011; Slochower, 1996, 2004).

At the outset, I want to emphasize that I do not believe that relational theory in general has necessarily minimized the particular kind of intersubjective revolution in psychoanalysis that Winnicott introduced. Writers such as Benjamin (1988, 1990) keyed into many specific elements of Winnicott's new ways of considering the infant/mother dyad, the roles of illusion and disillusionment, and the generative functions of destruction for playing and reality, even as she critiqued the limitations of Winnicott's conceptualization of maternal subjectivity. Slochower's (1996, 2004) translation of some parts of Winnicott's notion of holding (also see Bass, 1996) is also noteworthy, as is Grossmark's (2016) attempt to reconcile elements of Winnicott's holding concept with his ideas of analytic companioning. Both Ogden (2016) and I (2019; 2022) have elaborated elements of Winnicott's notion of destruction, both its creative elements in living and the ways in which the reactions of the object being destroyed are crucial to the movement from relating to usage.

In Mitchell's defense, when trying to underscore useful tendencies and trends it can be easy to overlook or minimize large differences. I would also defend Mitchell, along with Roy Schafer in 1983 and Greenberg and Mitchell (1983), since they were all in the early 1980s inventing comparative psychoanalytic theory in one way or another. As Schafer (1985, p. 277) said regarding comparative psychoanalysis, he strove toward being equally unfair to each theory. In the developmental tilt paper, Mitchell largely achieved this goal, but was not equally unfair in his consideration of Winnicott. Mitchell (1984) concludes his paper with a humble acknowledgment of the challenge of comparative theorizing when he states: "In theorizing as in living, no choice is without its price" (p. 497). In part, I think that my argument represents a wish that I could have continued my conversation with Mitchell about comparative psychoanalysis and, in particular, his developmental tilt hypothesis regarding Winnicott.

Mitchell's decision to lump Winnicott with the other theorists mentioned was to some extent understandable, in that in certain ways Winnicott tried to appear that he was not upsetting the Freudian apple cart. He was a political compromiser or even avoider of conflict. Winnicott did, through some sleight of hand, try to advertise himself as preserving elements of Freudian theory while disavowing Freud's unique contributions.

For example, it is stunning to read Winnicott and Khan's (1953) review of Fairbairn's new book, "Studies in Personality." They are quite critical of Fairbairn's rejection of drive theory despite the fact that one can see considerable overlap between their shared assertions regarding a drive toward object relating. Winnicott wanted to seem less revolutionary than he was, while developing a whole new way of viewing infantile and child development as well as clinical psychoanalysis. Winnicott created a revolution in thinking about intersubjectivity, the role of illusion, our ways of thinking about destruction and aggression, and how we think about the very essence of psychoanalytic process and therapeutic action.

Mitchell's objection to the other theories is on the theoretical grounds that their innovations in theory preserved drive as a central construct. In contrast, Winnicott introduced major changes in theory while trying to obfuscate it in disclaimers. This is a different matter than whether he developed his theory in accord with Mitchell's hypothesis.

Mitchell (1984) makes reference to only two of Winnicott's papers, one of which is a bizarre and obscure paper on birth trauma and the other on regression. While Mitchell clearly understood much about the weight of Winnicott's achievements (e.g. Greenberg and Mitchell, 1983), it has taken many analysts a long time to fully grasp that what Winnicott and Bion were doing was inventing a completely new way of thinking about analysis. Throughout Mitchell's writing in the 1984 paper and beyond (e.g. Mitchell, 2000) is his concern with psychoanalysts' tendency to use developmental metaphors in infantilizing patients. I believe that this important concern was largely responsible for Mitchell's relative lack of emphasis on Winnicott's most revolutionary contributions to the understanding of intersubjectivity.

Mitchell also fails to mention both the central element of Winnicott's vision, that of play, and the problems that play assists us with—those of parsing inside and outside as enduring problems as a part of living. As late as 2000, Mitchell continues to refer to Winnicott primarily in critical terms regarding his "obfuscation" (p. 80) of the ways that he was changing psychoanalytic theory. Mitchell repeated his developmental tilt hypothesis that Winnicott reserved most of his innovations for false self-disorders, preserving more classical formulations for the neurosis. Mitchell is not without contradiction, though, crediting Winnicott (1945, p. 101) with "illuminating the subtle ways in which secure attachment facilitates the development of a secure sense of self." Here Mitchell seems to be acknowledging Winnicott's description of the facilitating environment in the context of normal development.

What is clear, though, is that even in 2000, Mitchell does not take up Winnicott's theory of play as a description of therapeutic action for all patients. Mitchell also fails to consider Winnicott's discussion of development as related to "capacities" (e.g. the capacity to be alone or the capacity for concern). In both these regards, Mitchell has fortified his developmental tilt hypothesis while minimizing the radical contributions that Winnicott was making to the understanding of intersubjectivity and the therapeutic action of psychoanalysis itself.

Winnicott was simply a different kind of theorist than those that Mitchell critiqued, and a unique theorist in relation to those who have come after. Central to Winnicott's theory were many elements of the life-long challenge of finding play in relation to inner and outer as well as reality and fantasy. He introduced play as the center of therapeutic activity and therapeutic action—as something that helped integrate the persistent enigmatic challenges of parsing inside and outside. Finally, he was also a fundamentally "ontologically" oriented analyst (e.g. Ogden, 2019; Cooper, 2021, 2022). This set him apart from epistemologically oriented analysts, such as Klein and Freud, and maybe even to some extent many contemporary analysts, including Mitchell.

In this chapter, I will develop a few ways that Winnicott's body of work never fit into Mitchell's developmental tilt hypothesis, and why this matters. While it is largely beyond the scope of this chapter, I believe that a deep appreciation for the undergirding of Winnicott's project allows for a better understanding of the overlap and differences between relational theory and the independent tradition.

I will focus on several major points. First, Winnicott was often trying to elaborate life-long developmental tasks of distinguishing between the subjectively conceived object and the objectively perceived other. Winnicott continually makes the argument that transitional objects are neither internalized, repressed, nor mourned and are instead diffused into cultural experience, religion, and the arts. Once again, the task of a person is to live with the enduring challenges of separating me from not-me possessions and inside from outside reality.

Second, Winnicott's theory of play (1968b) is based on elements of symmetrical relatedness between patient and analyst. This does not fit neatly into Mitchell's thesis that Winnicott could be grouped with theorists such as Kernberg, Kohut, Modell, Klein, and Hartmann who focused exclusively on the importance of the earliest, most regressive elements of experience. Mitchell does not mention either the central element of Winnicott's vision—that of play—or the way that play assists us with problems as we live our lives rather than being strictly consigned to the earliest parts of life.

Winnicott's theory of destruction related to the generative elements of destructiveness in discovering reality. Winnicott's theory of aggression itself is that aggression is not only reactive to the loss of a gratifying environment but that we are developmentally wired to experience a curiosity about the object world, expressed through motility itself. The characterization of Winnicott as organized around provision and "being a good object" (Mitchell, 1984, p. 479) or "replacement object" (p. 489) also seems to me to be a significant misunderstanding of Winnicott's theory and theory of technique that I will explore.

Winnicott (1968a) redefined interpretation as a kind of responsiveness, a way of helping the patient to be and become who they are rather than to primarily understand and know themselves. This process of being and becoming, one that also overlaps with elements of the existentialist current in parts of psychoanalysis, (e.g. Slavin, 2016) is the antithesis of reducing human existence and psychoanalysis to the persistence of early object relational fixations. Instead, Winnicott saw that the problems of parsing the internal with externality was part of being human, part of learning to play with the enduring, enigmatic puzzle of being a person with other persons. It is "the place where we live" (Winnicott, 1968) and it is the very essence of how play helps us to live and work in the seam between these two realms. In my view, this form of playing also has in the background that we are each playing with borrowed time.

Winnicott as a Theorist Who Emphasized the Continuity and Perpetuity of Psychic Engagement

One of Mitchell's central theses in his developmental tilt article is the notion that theorists such as Fairbairn, Guntrip, Kohut, Kernberg, Modell, and Winnicott preserved Freud's understanding of the mind in terms of conflicts among drives while relegating the development of object relations to an earlier period in development. Mitchell (1984, p. 477) states:

> Despite this diversity in degrees of fealty, each author requires accommodation to make room for his or her own contribution, and therefore many of these innovations have been introduced into psychoanalytic theory via the developmental tilt; conse-quently, the dynamic issues they depict tend to get characterized as infantile, pre-oedipal, immature, and their persistence in later life is often regarded as a residue of infantilism, rather than as an expression of human relational needs extending throughout the life cycle.

Mitchell neither emphasized nor even mentioned that Winnicott's task of distinguishing between the subjectively conceived object and the objectively perceived other positions him as a theorist who was not tucking psychic developmental tasks into what Mitchell referred to as "an infinite regress" (p. 489).

For Winnicott, "playing and reality" (Winnicott, 1971) are em-bedded in constant dialogue, conflict, and transformation in the continuous process of living. While many people focus on play as the opposite of what is serious, for Winnicott the opposite of play is what is real—that is, reality. Benjamin (1990) suggested in her reading of Winnicott, and I agree, that the child's fascination with what is outside (not just their conflict with reality as in the reality principle) is continuous with our appreciation of externality. Intrinsically, play involves transit (e.g. Cooper, 2019; Corbett, 2017) between un-represented and represented experience, between what is familiar and what is unfamiliar, and between interiority and alterity.

Winnicott emphasized the persistence of early object relational stages into adulthood not as fixations but rather as part of being a human being. Let's look first at the transitional object concept. One of the most important things that Winnicott (1951) stressed in the transitional object paper is that the transitional object is neither re-pressed nor mourned. Instead, the transitional object is diffused into cultural experience, religion and the arts. Once again, the task of a person is to live with the enduring challenges of separating me from not-me possessions and inside from outside reality. Nor is the tran-sitional object, as some self psychologists argued (e.g. Tolpin, 1971), internalized as a form of psychic structure through transmuting internalizations. For Winnicott, the objects that we make use of, whether they are the objects that help us with the first me/not-me possession (e.g. transitional objects) or the objects that help us dif-ferentiate between relating to objects and using objects, are there to be made use of during our lifetime. Instead of repressing, mourning, or internalizing the transitional object, we engage with transitional phenomena in living and playing. Thus, Winnicott proposed that the fate of the transitional object is that it is diffused into cultural, artistic and religious experiences.

While Winnicott discusses the problems and consequences asso-ciated with not being met by a transitional object (e.g. not having an available transitional object during separation or having one foisted on the child too early), it cannot be emphasized enough that for Winnicott, human existence revolves around the enduring presence of necessary illusion and working/playing with those illusions. So, one of the most revolutionary ideas in Winnicott's work (at the time) was that he wasn't relegating object relational matters exclusively to early periods of life.

Winnicott's two papers on culture during the period of 1968–1971 develop many of his earlier ideas on transitional objects, transitional phenomena, and potential space and are relevant to my argument. It was also during this period that he emphasized the importance of culture as a way to continue to find play and work on the problem of what is inside and outside. In his magnificent paper "The Place

Where We Live," he addresses a psychoanalytic view of culture that goes far beyond traditional concepts of sublimation. In so doing, he announced more directly his critique of Freud's views on culture, siding with Trilling's observation that Freud held an "ambivalence" (Trilling, 1959) about the concept of culture. For Winnicott, culture is intrinsic "to the place where we live" because it exists in transitional space. And transitional space is always and forever.

In "The Place Where We Live," Winnicott raises this question: "Here are two places, then, the inside and outside of the individual but is this all?" Winnicott was highly unsatisfied that most psychoanalytic writing influenced by Freud dwelled either on the individual's relationship to objects or else on the inner life of the individual. Winnicott raises the question of where we are when we take in art or engage in sports. While he is profoundly interested in what we are doing (e.g. playing and using, which comprise a great deal of the final phase of his psycho-analytic writing), in this essay he raises the question: where are we when we are doing, "if we are anywhere at all" (p. 222)?

Winnicott felt that psychoanalysis had never addressed the matter of how the experiences of the individual person (baby, child, adult) in-teracting with the environment result in playing and cultural experi-ence. He felt the need for a third concept beyond the concept of inner and outer, suggesting potential space as the place for creative playing and for cultural experience to occur. Potential space is the hypothetical area between the baby and the object mother during the phase of the repudiation of the object as not-me, as merger with the mother is concluded. He identifies a special feature of the place where play and cultural experience occur, not as fixation but in ways that depend on "living experiences, not on inherited tendencies" (p. 225). Winnicott is continually interested in where and how play occurs.

Mitchell's Characterization of Winnicott as Proposing "Simple" Provision

Mitchell (1984, p. 489), in reference to Winnicott, Guntrip, Balint, and Kohut stated that:

> Needs are developmental necessities; the child requires certain kinds of parenting behaviors to provide necessary experiences. If

the parent provides them, the child continues to develop; if the parent does not provide them, the child stops developing, becomes frozen. Similarly, if the analyst does not provide these object relational opportunities in some fashion, nothing else can happen. It is not gratification of impulses; it is a question of reaching the self by providing necessary experiences. Serious psychopathology, in Winnicott's view, is always a result of inadequate provision of needs, always an "environmental deficiency disease." In Winnicott's model, the simple provision of maternal functions produces in the child non-conflictual experience and the simple unfolding of the self.

Mitchell uses the word "simple" twice in ways that minimize the massive complexity of Winnicott's project. First, Winnicott was not saying that the child does not have conflictual experiences. He was for the first time saying that not all defenses are erected in response to "id" impulses, as the classical model of defense had suggested. He was trying to discuss patients whose parents were so unreliable regarding the presentation of reality (e.g. specious reality testing or serious narcissistic vulnerabilities) that reality could not be trusted. In these cases, patients needed to erect defenses against objects, such as self-sufficiency or schizoid withdrawal (Modell, 1968; Winnicott, 1949). In fact, in these instances there is *a conflict* with the feeling of loving/needing/wanting to trust a parent and not trusting a parent that gives rise to the false self.

Mitchell's use of argumentation here also begs the question: Is there really any analyst of any persuasion who would argue that there is something called "a non-conflictual experience?" Winnicott's theory of the generative elements of "destructiveness" suggested that destruction enables the transition from an entirely subjectively perceived other (relating) to an entity that is objectively perceived as existing outside the self. As Benjamin (1990) underscored, Winnicott's theory of destructiveness suggests a basic tension or conflict between omnipotence and recognition of reality, between denial and affirmation of the other.

The use of the term "simple" to describe "simple maternal functions" to facilitate growth is also painting with too broad a brushstroke. Winnicott used the term "giving back" in reference to interpretation, which is a much more subtle and nuanced concept than it may sound. Winnicott was always concerned that interpretations, whether they focused on conflict, defense, unconscious fantasy or transference, were liable to become highly intellectualized or foster indoctrination of the patient. He sought to find play in the places where the patient's unconscious mind provided openings, what Green (1975) referred to as "ventilated spaces." He was much more impressed by the patient's capacity to arrive at new experiences and insights in contrast to the analyst's formulations. Here Bion (1963) and Winnicott overlap with regard to Bion's concepts of selected fact and overvalued idea.

Mitchell's argument is also stretched in reference to Winnicott when he states that "The analyst must enter at the point of the environmental failure" (p. 489), providing relational experiences as "replacements" for those experiences which the infant never encountered. Here, Mitchell wants to focus on "replacement" as opposed to the notion of being met by an object who will facilitate doing something different with developmental failures. The very concept of playing is related to working with what has previously been conflictual and unresolved. I have argued that Winnicott's concept of play picked up from Freud's (1913) observation that the transference is enacted before it can be verbalized (Cooper, 2018). I argued that playing is what allows for the transformation of unsymbolized experiences into representation.

Winnicott's theory of play is based on elements of symmetrical relatedness between patient and analyst. His theory does not fit neatly into Mitchell's thesis that Winnicott could be grouped with theorists such as Kernberg, Kohut, Modell, Klein, and Hartmann, who focused exclusively on the importance of the earliest, most regressive elements of experience. While Winnicott conceptualized the analyst as a supervisor of play who managed the setting, it was essential that the analyst was also a participant in play. Here the symmetrical and asymmetrical elements of the analytic relationship are joined in a constant tension, sense of paradox, and generative play. I have suggested in a group of recent papers (e.g. Cooper, 2018, 2019) that play with what is old and new, with internalized and external objects, is born of conflict. I view this perspective as consistent with some unelaborated aspects of Winnicott's theory of play.

In fact, one of the major implications of his theory of play, and the analyst as a participant in play, was the focus on many elements of symmetry in the analytic situation. Among a few others, Ferenczi (1928) had also highlighted these elements of symmetry, but Winnicott's theory of play, which involves the analyst as participant and supervisor of play, basically introduced a model of therapeutic action that revolved around symmetry.

Let's look more specifically at Winnicott's (1968) view of interpretation in his less well known "Interpretation in Psychoanalysis." Winnicott emphasizes how frequently interpretations in psychoanalysis do not reach the patient and instead function as explanations that are abstract and satisfy the analyst's need to be helpful. In my speculations, some of the most abstract interpretations that Winnicott had in mind were those involving reconstruction of regressive, early experiences.

Winnicott suggests that the best types of interpretations "give back to the patient what the patient has communicated" (p. 254). By giving back the interpretation to the patient, the patient is enabled to correct misunderstandings. The analyst holds potential space in the analytic situation; in a sense, *the giving back of interpretation preserves the setting of analysis.* There is a place for the patient to become who he is; to play with the feelings, thoughts, and words he has spoken and that the analyst has spoken. There is a place to live, play and make use of the patient's being. It is a place where patient and analyst are always in a state of becoming. This view of psychoanalysis seems to me to be the opposite of Mitchell's (1984, p. 489) assertion that Winnicott's theory conceptualizes a "passive patient." Are analysts in other models who supply patients with interpretations encouraging passivity? Does conceptualizing analysis as a kind of squiggle game feature a passive patient? The matter of a passive/active dimension in analytic work simply cannot be summarized as one thing or other. It seems to me that much of Winnicott's views on clinical work emphasized the patient's active participation despite the fact that natural elements of regression were a part of his conceptual framework.

An even more subtle and brilliant theme of his chapter on interpretation is the humanistic and ontological view of what an interpretation is and how it functions in analysis. Winnicott's views on interpretation help us to understand "The Use of the Object." Winnicott's "Interpretation in Psychoanalysis" is essentially his view of how the patient makes use of the analyst and how the analyst can make himself available for usage. Winnicott provides some examples of how he is able to make some remarkably attuned comments about how patients and analysts work together. He discusses how patients learn the interpretive style of their analysts (including how their analysts may intellectualize and get ahead of the patient in doing so). Winnicott is really discussing how patients can or cannot "make use" of their analysts. Some patients work around their analyst's limitations in order to make use of them and some are less able to do so. Once again, the characterization of a "passive" patient as it relates to Winnicott's theory seems off the mark.

For Winnicott, interpretation has moved far outside the epistemological realm that is related to the content of unconscious conflict, defense, unconscious fantasy, internalized object relation, or interpersonal/relational configuration. In this paper, Winnicott is essentially asserting that all interpretations are a form of object relation and all object relations carry elements of interpretive understanding as well as anticipation of who the other is becoming. In his paper on interpretation, Winnicott has described a shift from epistemological approaches to interpretation related to knowing, to the notion that interpretations involve an experience between patient and analyst. Winnicott emphasizes that interpretation, the giving back to the patient of what he or she has said, occurs in real time. The patient is communicating within the reality of transference with all of the selective perception that that implies, and the analyst offers what he or she has heard in that moment, ideally something that is fresh. The patient receives what can be received within their varieties of dissociated states, defenses, or limited transference in a moment of time.

The concept of interpreting in real time does not fit neatly into Mitchell's characterization of a group of object relations theorists that are focused on an "infinite regress" (p. 479). In my view, each of these elements of Winnicott's work are quite the opposite of what Mitchell described as "collapsing relational issues into the interaction between the mother and infant during the earliest months of life" (p. 479).

When Mitchell noted object relations theorists' tendencies to focus on the patient's regressive tendencies, he was highlighting their minimization of some of the symmetrical elements of the analytic relationship. He did so partly to highlight the patient's capacities to know. Yet Winnicott was also noting in his ontological approach to analysis a shared existential space between patient and analyst in a way that Mitchell did not take into account in the developmental tilt hypothesis.

There is a vast territory between "replacement" on the one hand and valorizing the content of interpretation whether the focus is on the repetition of interpersonal patterns, drives, defense, or unconscious fantasy. Winnicott and the independent tradition in general (e.g. Parsons, 2009), following from Ferenczi's seminal (1928) paper on elasticity, highlight how much the patient has to offer by way of understanding, growth, and becoming who they are, rather than through the insights provided by the analyst. I don't believe that Winnicott was writing about replacing anyone.

More on Being a "Good Object or Replacement Object" and Play

While some theories related to the fate of the bad object suggest a kind of exorcism or "release" of the bad object (e.g. Fairbairn, 1952) through analytic work, Winnicott did not use the term "release." Perhaps he chose not to because the term "release" seems to turn a blind eye to how these objects nearly always endure as part of the internalized psychic economy of the individual. Does release mean loosened or entirely let go of? Winnicott, alternatively, elaborated the idea that psychoanalysis promotes greater capacities to play internally and externally with our enduring experiences of others. "Play" stands in contrast to "release" since play is contingent on the enduring internalized bad object and external object as play partners with the patient and analyst. This involves the patient's relation to his or her own internal world, the analyst's relation to his or her own internal world and the intersubjective experience of trying to know the patient's inner world together.

One of the most important parts of the analyst's subjectivity and complex participation in analytic work relates to the nature of play as the central component of therapeutic activity and therapeutic action. In play, one is never *simply* one thing or other and certainly not always a good object. What fun is that? The concept of "simple" is incompatible with play since if rules or circumstances of potential play are too homogeneous or rigidly held, the participants are not invited into imaginative engagement. Quite often finding play involves finding places of good enough friction. In fact, in intense projective identifications, the analyst is often being unconsciously asked to hold rigid, unchanging affects and attributes that make play hard to find.

While a great deal of psychoanalysis has focused on Winnicott's (1951) formulation of the "holding" elements of transitional space and play, I emphasize that the concept of limit was also, always, constitutive of play for Winnicott (Cooper, in press). Green (1975) elaborated the importance of limit in Winnicott's notion of the setting, a matter that has not always been a point of emphasis in conceptualizations of holding. From the beginning of Winnicott's writing, as is clear from his emphasis on the analyst's hate in the countertransference, the concept of limit was essential to understanding influential elements of the analytic setting in facilitating play (Winnicott, 1949). For example, Winnicott's (1945) understanding that the analyst of a depressed patient must cope with his own "guilt and grief resultant from the destructive elements of his own (the analyst's) love" (p. 147) implicitly recognized the concept of limit. The analyst must always work with the limits of his own relation to internal objects in order to understand the things the patient carries (Cooper, 2014; Corbett, 2014; Seligman, 2014).

Mitchell (1984) has reduced a complex analytic process elaborated by Winnicott into "the simple provision of maternal functions" (p. 479), while neglecting to mention some of the other functions that were intrinsic to Winnicott's conceptualization of the setting. Mitchell references an obscure paper by Winnicott about birth and prenatal experiences in order to buttress his general argument that for all of these object relations theorists, "deeper is transformed into earlier." Yet Winnicott addresses various elements of the analyst's subjectivity and holding functions in a number of different papers. Mitchell does not acknowledge that the problem of honoring or disrupting illusion is not consigned to the first few years of life, and that this problem is the very undergirding of a model of intersubjectivity at the center of Winnicott's project. That project is partly to describe how human beings work and play with illusion during their lifetime. The depth is there, always already, an idea that is at odds with "deeper is transformed into earlier."

Then there is hate in the countertransference in which Winnicott broke new ground by discussing countertransference at all and in particular the analyst's limits. In Primitive Emotional Development (Winnicott, 1945) there is discussion of the analyst's depression as a prerequisite to interpreting the patient's depression in the contemporariness of the analytic setting. It was after all the first time that an analyst was describing intergenerational transmission of depression as something to look out for in the interpersonal relationship between patient and analyst. And, as Ogden (2016) and I (Cooper, 2018) in separate papers have elucidated, it may very well be the analyst's response to the patient's destruction of the object which catalyzes the patient's movement from relating to usage, an idea that is almost axiomatic for many relational thinkers. And as discussed in Chapter 3, some elements of how the use of the analyst's limits in many clinical contexts is central to facilitating growth and mourning.

All of these add up to something much more complex than a parent/analyst acclimating to the patient and conceptualizing growth only in terms of that reductionistic characterization. But perhaps most important is that Mitchell's characterization of "simple provision" is missing the point that in an ontological approach, a squiggle game method of interpretation and giving back to the patient require different constructs than provision, replacement, and the active/passive axis. For Winnicott the intersubjective context of the analytic situation is dense and complex despite the fact that at the time, psychoanalysis had not yet made much use of elements of the analyst's explicit expressiveness.

Benjamin (1988) usefully drew our attention to the complex subjectivity of maternal responsiveness, elaborating elements that were unelaborated by Winnicott. Benjamin (1990) gives an astute, thorough-going conceptualization of Winnicott's concept of holding, one that goes beyond thinking of the analyst as exclusively acclimating to the needs of the patient. Slochower (1996, 2004) has also provided a useful exploration of the concept of holding. She juxtaposes certain versions of holding with the kinds of analyst-expressiveness and disclosure emphasized in relational theory (e.g. Bass, 1996). Her work is meaningful because it would be a stretch to say that Winnicott extensively elaborated elements of the analyst's subjectivity. On the other hand, it would be a mistake to think of Winnicott's version of holding as primarily eliding elements of the analyst's subjectivity, a point that Slochower has helped us to understand.

Consider this statement from Mitchell:

> The skewing of relational issues created by the developmental tilt is sometimes accompanied by two additional clinical emphases – a tendency to minimize the importance of conflict and a tendency to portray the patient as essentially passive. These two qualities characterize in particular, the clinical approaches developed by Winnicott, Guntrip, Balint, and Kohut.
>
> (p. 489)

While Winnicott was not fundamentally a conflict theorist, the idea that he conceptualizes the patient as "passive" is hard to reconcile with the theorist who discovered play as a part of therapeutic action and who redefined the analytic setting as a playground. It is the patient who brings the play when possible. It is the patient and analyst who participate in interpretive squiggle games. It is the patient who creatively destroys in order to generate new meanings and relationships with others.

In fact, while it has never been given sufficient attention, Winnicott placed great stock in the patient's capacity to direct analysis to where it needed to go. This trust in the patient, an essential part of his concept of holding, seems to me the opposite of fostering "passivity" as Mitchell characterized. Winnicott (1968, 1971), more than any analyst since Ferenczi (1928), viewed the patient as having to arrive at understanding and meaning, and believed that the analyst's chief role was not to supply knowledge but to facilitate play. King (1978) along with Parsons (2009) emphasized that Winnicott's view of holding is captured in the implicit hope and trust that can be implied in waiting, an idea that T. S. Eliot's poem "Wait Without Hope" explores.

For example, Winnicott's notion of the analyst's use of interpretation to express the limits of understanding is quite nuanced in how it sees the analyst's communication with the patient and his concept of holding. Winnicott believed that it was the psychoanalytic setting that allowed patients to better become who they are. Interpretations serve the setting not by importing knowledge but by underscoring the setting as a place where play might be discovered. Mitchell's characterization of the patient as passive within Winnicott's theory is difficult to re-concile with so many elements of how Winnicott conceptualized clinical work and the role of the patient in that work.

For Winnicott, analytic authority and the valorization of traditional interpretation (whether the referent point be defense, conflict, or relational configurations) was not all it was cracked up to be. For analysts such as Mitchell (1984), Hoffman (1983, 1996), Stern (1997), and Cooper (1993), the chief complaint about epistemological approaches involved the questioning of the analyst's sovereign authority to know. They usefully explained that many forms of psychoanalysis ascribed analytic authority to the analyst rather than ceding it to the patient. But relational analysts have not always challenged the basic under-girding of epistemological approaches to psychoanalysis as a therapy based on the project of knowing and understanding. Many relationally oriented analysts have focused on the understanding of relational configurations while at the same time ceding to the patient a great deal of authority to partner with the analyst in these explorations. The epistemological tradition lives on in some versions of relational theory despite the emphasis on greater symmetry between patient and analyst.

I think that relational theory is probably best understood as bor-rowing from both the epistemological and ontological traditions. Analysts such as Levenson (1972, 1983), Bromberg (1996), and Stern (1997) represent strong elements of an ontological strand in relational theory.

Hoffman's (1996) interest in death and time carried out elements of existential psychoanalysis which is clearly related to the tradition of "being" in psychoanalysis. Slavin (2016) has compellingly linked re-lational thinking with existential concerns.

Both Winnicott and Bion focused more on helping patients with being and becoming than knowing and understanding. It is to Winnicott's different way of thinking about and doing psychoanalysis that I briefly turn with regard to Mitchell's developmental tilt hypothesis.

A Note about Winnicott's Ontological Psychoanalysis and the Developmental Tilt

A recent paper by Ogden (2019) characterized four psychoanalytic theorists—Freud, Klein, Winnicott, and Bion—as best understood as primarily either epistemologically or ontologically oriented. Ogden (2019) accurately drew attention to the ways that both Winnicott through play and Bion through dreaming invented new ways of working than the epistemological approaches of both Freud and Klein.

Ogden suggests, and I agree, that Winnicott is not even best understood as an object relations theorist at all. He notes that it was rare for Winnicott to mention internalized objects. That matter is less important than the observation that Winnicott was inventing an entirely new way of even thinking about psychoanalysis, an ontological approach in contrast to the epistemological approaches developed by Freud and Klein.

The matter of clearly differentiating between the two traditions is complex and any sort of binary between epistemological and ontological approaches falters in a reductionistic theoretical cul-de-sac (see Chapter 6). Foehl (2010) has suggested that our "theoretical encrustations" may in fact sometimes complicate understanding clinical process more than clarify it. I would suggest that most analyses, regardless of theoretical orientation, include elements of both the epistemological and ontological elements. For example, knowing another person may often facilitate becoming more oneself, and being—or discovering how to be—with another person may facilitate knowing better who one is and is becoming.

Winnicott's project of thinking about interpretation in the ways that he did is interesting to think about in relation to Hannah Arendt's (1996) definition of love, one that she borrowed from St. Augustine. Arendt (1958, 1996) defined love as, "I want you to be" (p. 9). In psychoanalysis, "I want you to be" is always complicated by the fact that patients are often trying to change their way of being and want to become something potentially a bit, or a lot, different. Countertransference tells us that we as analysts cannot promise that we always want our patients to be as they are, no matter how much we might wish for that. For example, Benjamin's (1988) critique of the developmental model of Winnicott was useful in drawing our attention to the complex subjectivity of maternal responsiveness related to limit.

I believe that it is possible to link Winnicott's notion that we interpret primarily to show our patients the limits of our understanding with the recognition of limitations of the analyst in wanting and facilitating our patients in becoming who they are. These include not only the limits of how much we can know and understand our patient but also how much we can be aware of our own complex subjectivity. Holding involves a way of holding that ambiguity and mysteriousness with ourselves and our patients. I think of Winnicott as essentially arguing that interpretation is an enactment of a form of compromise—a compromise between the wish to offer and the limitation in doing so, the wish to understand and the limitation in doing so, the wish to understand the patient's communication and non-communication (Winnicott, 1963) the wish to help the patient to be and the limitation in doing so.

By no means was the area of the analyst's complex subjectivity, including limit and excitement, flushed out in theoretical terms by Winnicott. It has been partially better understood both by contemporary Independent tradition analysts such as Symington (1983) and Parsons (2000, 2006, 2007) and relationally oriented analysts such as Bass (1996), Bromberg (1996), Davies (2003), Benjamin (1988, 2004), and Slochower (1996).

Concluding Remarks

Mitchell's (1984) developmental tilt paper remains a seminal paper in the history of relational thinking. His discussion of Winnicott's work, however, it is too reductionistic, selectively minimizing several of the most important elements of his contributions. I have suggested that Winnicott, as such a unique theorist and the progenitor of some of the most important dimensions of intersubjectivity, really stands outside Mitchell's critique. While he is better known for his many articles charting early development, Winnicott's use of play as the center of analytic process created early forms of ontological psychoanalysis.

I hope that analysts trained primarily in the relational model, and all models, will learn a view of Winnicott that is focused on understanding the complexity of his models of holding and responsiveness. For this to happen, it is important to not contrast "holding" with the idea of the analyst's expressiveness. The analyst's participation and expressiveness are useful dimensions of work, and obviously, analytic expressiveness is intrinsic to the analytic process. Holding is not the opposite of analytic expressiveness.

The developmental tilt critique of some elements of object relations theory usefully pointed out that many theories focused more exclusively on the impact of the first few years of life while still trying to preserve Freud's original drive theory. In some ways, though, Mitchell's critique of the developmental tilt may have also steered us away from the intrinsic developmental components in the psychoanalytic process. Mitchell's critique helped many analysts to not valorize regression and instead to work with it as it arises. We need to always be aware of when regression is iatrogenic, just as we should be aware that regressive components of the analytic process can be natural, helpful, and even necessary. Sometimes our intellectualized interpretations may impede an analytic process from developing and gaining traction.

I have always felt that there was so much to gain from finding ways to integrate the work of Winnicott and the independent tradition with relational and interpersonal perspectives. There is far more overlap and shared ancestry (e.g. Ferenczi) than has been appreciated. In recent years, analysts have tried to describe more vividly the experiences of the analyst during some of the processes that Winnicott focused on, especially in his enigmatic and evocative tour de force, "The Use of the Object." Essentially, authors such as Bromberg (1996), Ogden (2004, 2016), Roussillon (2011), Fabozzi (2016), and Cooper (2018, 2019, in press a, b, c) have described not only the analyst's experience in the process of destruction of the object but also the impact of their experience on the patient's ability to move from relating to object usage.

Mitchell's ability to draw attention to the ways that object relational theories split off interpersonal relating from the early development of object relations was quite heuristically helpful. Unfortunately, by minimizing the existential and ontological elements of Winnicott's revolutionary contributions, we have not yet fully utilized the benefits of a marriage of "talking about what's going on around here" (Levenson, 1972, 1983) with "helping patients to be" (Chapter 6).

The notion of Hannah Arendt's (1958, 1961, 1996) definition of love, "I want you to be," is a most complex project for any analytic treatment and comes pretty close to what Winnicott was inventing in clinical psychoanalysis. In wanting to help our patients to be, there is no circumventing the idea that they are the products of how they were helped and not helped during development. To facilitate being and becoming, we do have to learn about, find, and live with what is in the way. Understanding these places of interruption need not be at odds with some of the important contributions of relational and interpersonal theory. Hopefully, a tilt toward development, need no longer be associated with the theoretical maneuver to preserve drive theory, as Mitchell exposed so persuasively. Psychoanalytic theory, like the psychoanalytic process itself, sometimes tilts one way and then we realize that we have tilted too far. To be human is to tilt, and sometimes, to tilt too far.

Note

1 Sections of this chapter first appeared in *Psychoanalytic Dialogues* 31: 3.

References

Arendt, H. (1958) *The Human Condition*. Chicago: The University of Chicago Press.

Arendt, H. (1961) *Between Past and Future*. London: Faber and Faber Limited.

Arendt, H. (1996) *Love and Saint Augustine*, ed. Joanna Vecchiarelli Scott and Judith Chelius Stark. Chicago: The University of Chicago Press.

Bass, A. (1996) Holding, holding back, and holding on. Commentary on paper by Joyce Slochower. *Psychoanal. Dial.* 6: 361–378.

Benjamin, J. (1988) *The Bonds of Love: Psychoanalysis, Feminism, and the Problem of Domination*. New York: Pantheon Books.

Benjamin, J. (1990) An outline of intersubjectivity: The development of recognition. *Psychoanal. Psychol.* 7S(Supplement): 33–46.

Benjamin, J. (2004) Beyond doer and done to. An Intersubjective View of Thirdness. *Psychoanal. Q.* 73(1): 5–46.

Bion, W. (1963) *Learning from Experience*. London: London: Rowman and Littlefield.

Bromberg, P. M. (1996) *Standing in the Spaces: Essays on Clinical Process, Trauma and Dissociation*. Hillsdale, NJ: The Analytic Press.

Cooper, S. H. (1993) Interpretive fallibility and the psychoanalytic dialogue. *J. Amer. Psychoanal. Int. J. Psycho-Anal.* 41: 95–126.

Cooper, S. H. (2000) Mutual containment in the analytic situation. *Psychoanal. Dial.* 10: 169–194.

Cooper, S. H. (2014) The things we carry: Finding/creating the object and the analyst's self-reflective participation. *Psychoanal. Dial.* 24: 621–636.

Corbett, K. (2017) Transit: Playing the other. Paper given at Psychology and the Other Conference, Boston.

Cooper, S. H. (2018) Playing in the darkness: Use of the object and use of the subject. *J. Amer. Psychoanal. Assn.* 66(4): 743–765.

Cooper, S. H. (2019) A theory of the setting: The transformation of un-represented experience and play. *Int. J. Psycho-Anal.* 100: 1439–1454.

Cooper, S. H. (2021) Toward an ethic of play. *Psychoanal. Q.* 90: 373–397.

Cooper, S. H. (2022) Inside, outside, playing and using in perpetuity: An essay on Winnicott's work from 1967–1968. *J. Amer. Psychoanal. Assn.* 70: 187–193.

Corbett, K. (2014) The analyst's private space: Spontaneity, ritual, psy-chotherapeutic action, and self-care. *Psychoanal. Dial.* 24(6): 637–647.

Davies, J. M. (2003) Falling in love with love: Oedipal and postoedipal manifestations of idealization and erotic masochism. *Psychoanal. Dial.* 13: 1–27.

Fabozzi, P. (2016) The use of the analyst and the sense of being real: The clinical meaning of Winnicott's "The Use of an Object". *Psychoanal. Q.* 85(1): 1–34.

Fairbairn, R. (1952) *Studies in Personality.* New York: Basic Books.

Ferenczi, S. (1928/1955) The elasticity of psycho-analytic technique. Reprinted, *Final Contributions to the Problems and Methodls of Psychoanalysis* (pp. 87–101). London: Hogarth. (Originally published, 1928)

Foehl, J. C. (2010) The play's the thing: The primacy of process and the per-sistence of pluralism in contemporary psychoanalysis. *Contemp. Psychoanal.* 46: 48–86.

Freud, S. (1913) Remembering, repeating and working through. *S.E.* 12: 145–157.

Green, A. (1975) The analyst, symbolization, and absence in the analytic setting – in memory of D. W. Winnicott. *Int. J. Psycho-Anal.* 56: 9–22.

Greenberg, J. and Mitchell, S. A. (1983) *Object Relations in Psychoanalytic Theory.* Cambridge, MA: Harvard University Press.

Grossmark, R. (2016) Psychoanalytic companioning. *Psychoanal. Dial.* 26(6): 698–712.

Hoffman, I. Z. (1983) The patient as interpreter of the analyst's experience. *Contemp. Psychoanal.* 19: 389–422.

Hoffman, I. Z. (1996) The intimate and ironic authority of the psycho-analytic experience. *Psychoanal. Q.* 65: 102–136.

King, P. (1978) Affective responses of the analyst to the patient's communications. *Int. J. Psychoanal.* 59: 329–334.

Levenson, E. A. (1972) *The Fallacy of Understanding. An Inquirty in the Changing Structure of Psychoanalysis.* New York: Basic Books.

Levenson, E. A. (1983) *The Ambiguity of Change.* New York: Basic Books.

Mitchell, S. (1984) Object relations theories and the developmental tilt. *Contemp. Psychoanal.* 20: 473–499.

Mitchell, S. (2000) *Relationality.* Hillsdale, NJ: The Analytic Press.

Mitchell, S. and Greenberg, J. (1983) *Object Relations Theory in Psychoanalytic Theory.* Cambridge: Harvard University Press.

Modell, A. (1968) *Object Love and Reality.* New York: International Universities Press.

Ogden, T. H. (2004) On holding and containing, being and dreaming. *Int. J. Psychoanal.* 85(6): 1349–1364.

Ogden, T. H. (2016) Destruction reconceived: On Winnicott's 'The Use of an Object and Relating through Identifications'. *Int. J. Psycho-Anal.* 97(5): 1243–1262.

Ogden, T. H. (2019) Ontological psychoanalysis or "What do you want to be when you grow up?" *Psycho. Q.* 88: 661–684.

Parsons, M. (1999). The logic of play in psychoanalysis. *Int. J. Psycho-Anal.* 80(5): 871–884.

Parsons, M. (2000) *The Dove That Returns, the Dove that Vanishes: Paradox and Creativity in Psychoanalysis.* London: Routledge.

Parsons, M. (2006) The analyst's countertransference to the analytic process. *Int. J. Psychoanal.* 87: 1183–1198.

Parsons, M. (2007) Raiding the inarticulate: The internal analytic setting and listening to countertransference. *Int. J. Psychoanal.* 88: 1441–1456.

Parsons, M (2009) An independent theory of clinical technique. *Psychoanal. Dial.* 19: 221–236.

Pizer, S. A. (1996) The negotiation of paradox in the analytic process. *Psychoanal. Dial.* 2: 215–240.

Roussillon, R. (2011) *Primitive Agony and Symbolization.* London: Routledge.

Seligman, S. (2014) Paying attention and feeling puzzled: The analytic mindset as an agent of therapeutic change. *Psychoanal. Dial.* 24(6): 648–662.

Schafer, R. (1985) Wild analysis. *J. Amer. Psychoanalytic Assn.* 33: 275–299.

Slavin, M. O. (2016) Relational psychonanalaysis and the tragic-existential aspect of the human condition. *Psychoanal. Dial.* 26: 537–548.

Slochower, J. (1996) Holding and the fate of the analyst's subjectivity. *Psychoanal. Dial.* 6: 323–353.

Slochower, J. (2004) *Holding and Psychoanalysis: A Relational Approach.* Hillsdale, NJ: The Analytic Press.

Stern, D. B. (1997) *Unformulated Experience: From Dissociation to Imagination in Psychoanalysis.* Hillsdale, NJ: The Analytic Press.

Symington, N. (1983) The analyst's act of freedom as agent of therapeutic change. *Int. R. Psycho-Anal.* 10: 283–291.

Tolpin, M. (1971) On the beginnings of a cohesive self—an application of the concept of transmuting internalization to the study of the transitional object and signal anxiety. *Psychoanal. Study of the Child* 26: 316–352.

Trilling, L. (1959) Freud and the crisis of our culture. *Amer. Imago.* 16: 73–75.

Winnicott, D. W. (1945) Primitive emotional development. In: *Through Paediatrics in Psychoanalysis* (pp. 145–156). New York: Basic Books.

Winnicott, D. W. (1949) Hate in the countertransference. In: *Through Paediatrics in Psychoanalysis* (pp. 194–203). New York: Basic Books.

Winnicott, D.W. and Khan, M. (1953) Review of Fairbairn's studies in personality. *Int. J. Psychoanal.* 34:312–317.

Winnicott, D. W. (1963) Communicating and not communicating, leading to study of certain opposites. In: *The Maturational Processes and the Facilitating Environment* (pp. 179–193). New York: International University Press.

Winnicott, D. W. (1968a) Interpretation in psychoanalysis. Originally published in C. Winnicott, R. Shepherd, & M. Davis (Eds.) (1989) *Psychoanalytic Explorations* (pp. 207–212). Cambridge, MA: Harvard University Press. Also in *The Collected Works of D. W. Winnicott,* ed. L. Caldwell and H. T. Robinson (pp. 253–257).

Winnicott, D. W. (1968b) Playing: Its theoretical status in the clinical situation. *Int. J. Psycho-Anal.* 49: 591–599.

Winnicott, D. W. (1971) The place where we live. In: *Playing and Reality* (pp. 104–110). London: Tavistock; (1968) The place where we live. *The Collected Works of D. W. Winnicott,* ed. L. Caldwell and H. T. Robinson (pp. 221–227).

Index

For Product Safety Concerns and Information please contact our EU
representative GPSR@taylorandfrancis.com
Taylor & Francis Verlag GmbH, Kaufingerstraße 24, 80331 München, Germany

9 781032 207551